Minimal Architecture

Architecture in Focus

Ilka & Andreas Ruby Angeli Sachs Philip Ursprung

Minimal Architecture

Prestel
Munich · Berlin · London · New York

Contents

Minimalism and Minimal Art

Philip Ursprung

For almost forty years artists, architects, critics and art historians have been racking their brains for a definition of minimalism. Is it a style? Is it the description of a cultural logic, i.e. an aesthetic approach extending across different fields that include art, architecture, music, fashion design and the critical discourse? Or does the term minimalism describe a range of design elements that are available everywhere and at all times such as the reduction to primary geometric forms, the right angle, the industrial "look" or the modular structure?

For us minimalism is a projection surface for ideas, a kind of playing field on which, since the mid-1960s—when the term was coined in New York—art and architecture have engaged each other in changing formations. The aim of this book is therefore not to pin down the meaning of the term minimalism but rather to examine the area where it is applied, to illuminate it and open it up to current architectural discussion. We have no wish to barricade ourselves behind apparently fixed definitions but prefer to adopt particular positions and to present our viewpoints for discussion. Our concern is not to underpin old clichés but to sharpen the perception of relationships and contradictions in contemporary architecture. The architects and projects we have selected may surprise a number of readers. Several of the prominent positions generally regarded in present-day architecture as typically minimalist, such as Alberto Campo Baeza or John Pawson, are not included in the project section at all while others we have chosen, such as Dominique Perrault or OMA Office for Metropolitan Architecture, have never previously been regarded from this viewpoint.

A Genuinely American Phenomenon

The idea of minimalism in the architectural discourse of the 1980s and 1990s separated itself by and large from the Minimal Art debate. If any similarities between buildings and interiors and certain aspects of Minimal Art are recorded then these are at most formal affinities. In the symposium held in the Royal Academy of Arts in London in 1998 the names of the most important minimal artists[1] were mentioned but, with few exceptions, the participants did not refer to concrete artworks or to the theory of the 1960s. In order to reactivate the discussion and to prevent it sinking to level of what Charles Jencks in London polemically described as "boutique Cistercianism"[2]— "Minimalism lends itself to spirituality but it also lends itself to shopping"[3]—a look at the history of art is certainly justified.

Donald Judd, one-person show, Green Gallery, New York 1963. Photograph by Rudolph Burckhardt.

Frank Stella, one-person exhibition of *Irregular Polygons*, Leo Castelli Gallery, New York 1966.

For the term minimalism, whatever way we understand it, is certainly rooted in Minimal Art, i.e. a subject that can be precisely located in art history.[4]

From my point of view there are two clichés that lead to the stagnation of the current architectural discussion. Firstly the confusion of Minimal Art with reductionism in the sense used in European modernism, secondly the idea that there is an naturally given affinity between Minimal Art and architecture. As it is simpler to deal with the first problem that is where I shall start. In her introduction to the London symposium Maggy Toy refers to the "removal of ornament" in the sense of Adolf Loos' text "Ornament und Verbrechen".[5] Under the term minimal architecture Peter Murray understands the "reduction of architecture to its most basic concepts of space, light and mass",[6] indeed he introduces the discussion with Mies' dictum "less is more".[7] In Anatxu Zabalbeascoas and Javier Rodriguez Marcos' book *Minimalisms* (2000) or Franco Bertoni's book *Architettura minimalista* (2002)[8] photos of buildings by Walter Gropius or Mies van der Rohe are placed beside illustrations of sculptures by Donald Judd, suggesting that Minimal Art functions as a kind of link between contemporary architecture and European high modernism as represented by Cubism, de Stijl or the Bauhaus movement.

In contrast it is my contention that Minimal Art is a genuinely American phenomenon inseparably linked to the flourishing New York art world of the mid-1960s. The Sixties was a decade of "new frontiers", the continual breaking down of barriers and apparently unstoppable economic, social and cultural growth. The decade was characterised by phenomenons such as sexual liberation and the civil rights movement but also by the claim to political dominance of the USA, which only reached its provisional limits at the beginning of the 1970s.[9] According to my way of thinking, to link the logic of Minimal Art to the theme of reduction is missing the point. It is far more closely related to spatial expansion as well as to the marking of new territories. It articulates a transition from the dominance of two-dimensionality to that of space, from painting to sculpture and from the object to the environment which characterised the artistic logic of the 1960s. By virtue of its flexible and additive structure Minimal Art is focussed entirely on growth and can be enlarged to almost any required degree. Gallery spaces soon become too small for this art, it expands in the shortest of time into public space, indeed at the end of the 1960s even into the desert regions of America—not as a form of criticism of the art world but as a sign of its triumph. In fact I would even maintain that Donald Judd's steel cubes arranged in modular rows, Dan Flavin's fluorescent tubes, Carl Andre's floor sculptures of bricks and metal plates, Robert Morris' installations and Sol LeWitt's grids mark, so to speak, the triumph of American sculpture over everything generally understood at that time as European modernist painting.

If one examines the sources from the Sixties it is remarkable that the protagonists of Minimal Art explicitly disassociated themselves from the European tradition. For example, in 1964 Judd stated polemically: "I'm totally uninterested in European art and I think it's over with."[10] He did not have much use for Mies' idea of "less is more": "I consider the Bauhaus too long ago to think about, and I never thought about it much."[11] Frank Stella said: "I find all that European geometric painting—sort of post-Max Bill school—a kind of curiosity—very dreary."[12] For Carl Andre Minimal Art meant the emancipation from the "cultural overload"[13] and for Robert Morris also the new order was "not based on previous art orders".[14]

Europe not only stood for a cultural inheritance which young American artists wished to overthrow but also for a rigid view of space that was questioned in the 1960s. Artists such as Robert Morris, who also appeared as a dancer and performer, set space in motion and formulated the relationship between artworks and their surroundings in a completely new way. To put it simply: the protagonists of Minimal Art took the paintings out of their frames and the sculptures down from their pedestals. For a "specific object", as Donald Judd termed the linking of painting and sculpture, or a shaped canvas by Frank Stella the entire gallery space becomes a plinth or a frame. Unlike the constructivist sculptures of Vladimir Tatlin or Max Bill's concrete sculptures the objects do not stand in an autonomous space that separates them from their surroundings, they take place in what Judd describes as "actual space". They share the space in which the viewer's body is also located. In other words: the effect of a minimalist artwork in an exhibition would vanish were one to place it in a frame or on a pedestal. And the most impressive photographs are those that do not isolate the minimalist art works but rather show them in their surroundings.

Although the protagonists of Minimal Art in the 1960s resisted attempts to catalogue them under a stylistic term they were unanimous in one essential point: for all of them the idea of composition was like a red rag to a bull. Instead of subordinating the internal structure of the artwork to a frame or a plinth they employed the serial addition of modules and elements, each of equal value and interchangeable. In 1940 the critic Clement Greenberg had compared Paul Klee's work with a limited inward growth, with cell division and increasing ramification that was at odds with the American impulse to cross boundaries[15]. Frank Stella emphasised that his art had absolutely nothing to do with the tradition of Malevitch, Mondrian or Bill as those artist were concerned with "composition" and "balance"—issues that no longer interested him. "The basis of their whole idea is balance. You do something in one corner and you balance it with something in the other corner."[16] Whereas such art is "relational", Stella described Minimal Art as "non-relational" and said: "The balance-factor isn't important."[17] And according to Robert Morris the ingredients of Minimal Art are "Symmetry, the lack of traces of process, abstractness, nonhierarchic distribution of parts, nonanthropomorphic orientations, general wholeness".[18]

For Donald Judd this new art revolved around categories such as "scale", "wholeness" and "directness". For Judd the whole was more important than the parts: "The whole is it. The big problem is to maintain the sense of the whole thing."[19] Where, as is the case in most of his works, a sculpture is made up of individual elements the impression should not be given that some are subordinate to or serve others. The whole should open up to the viewer right away. This idea has, incidentally, nothing to do with simplicity or reduction, categories which European architecture in the 1980s liked to associate with minimalism. Quite the contrary. The basic elements from which the art works are made may well be simple; the perception on the other hand is extremely complex. The stereotypical title "Untitled", given to a number of works of Minimal Art, has nothing to do with abstraction or absence of content but rather with the fact that it is impossible to adequately express their phenomenological diversity in language. While it is true that Dan Flavin uses standard shop-bought fluorescent tubes their visual effects in space, the play of light and shadow, the colour nuances and the changes in the corporeal perception of the viewer that they cause are so complex as to defy description. The rules according to which Sol LeWitt's grids are composed may well be simple but the form that results produces an endless number of views through and overlays. And although the grey-painted wooden structures that Robert Morris produced in the mid-1960s are apparently simple forms, for the viewer they produce confusing passageways, frames and platforms. "Simplicity of shape does not necessarily equate with simplicity of experience", as he said.[20] The issue for minimal artists was not to abstract things or simplify them. In Frank Stella's words "There's something awful about that

Dan Flavin, *"fluorescent light"*, Green Gallery, New York 1964. Photograph by Dan Flavin, Courtesy of Brydon Smith.

Sol LeWitt, one-person exhibition, Dwan Gallery, New York 1966.

Robert Morris, *Wheels*, 1963 (destroyed). Solomon Guggenheim Museum, New York.

Tony Smith, *Die*, 1962. Courtesy Paula Cooper Gallery, New York.

'economy of means.' I don't know why, but I resent that immediately. I don't go out of my way to be economical."[21] Donald Judd emphasised: "I object to the whole reduction idea, because it's only reduction of those things someone doesn't want. If my work is reductionist it's because it doesn't have the elements that people thought should be there. But it has other elements that I like."[22] And Sol LeWitt wrote: "The most interesting characteristic of the cube is that it is relatively uninteresting …Therefore it is the best form to use as a basic unit for any more elaborate function, the grammatical device from which the work may proceed."[23]

The idea of reduction was suspect to minimal artists largely because it lies at the centre of the modernist set of values. Another term for it is "essentialism", i.e. the idea that there exists such a thing as an essence or an inner being and that revealing or reaching this essence is the purpose of art and architecture. Instead of "essence" minimal artists prefer to talk of "presence". Indeed Minimal Art marks the transition from a genuine modernist search for the essential nature of art to the discussion of art's location. For them an artwork does not have to be "true" or "authentic", as was the case for their modernist predecessors, but above all "interesting". From the viewpoint of minimal artists the interest shown in the 1980s by architecture in authentic materials would have been an anachronism. Donald Judd's galvanised steel surfaces and Richard Artschwager's Formica veneers do not deal with authenticity but with artificiality. In the words of Frank Stella: "What you see is what you see."[24]

Minimal Art's Inclination Towards Architecture

As mentioned earlier it is more difficult to counter the second cliché namely that Minimal Art is linked to architecture by particularly close ties. In the first part of "Aspects of Minimal Architecture" (1994) an interior by Alberto Campo Baeza is placed opposite an illustration of Donald Judd's Chinati Foundation in Marfa, Texas.[25] The matter is all the more complicated as the assumption is not based merely on formal similarities such as large dimensions, the use of industrial materials and the delegation of the production but also on statements by minimal artists. In fact in the 1980s and 1990s Donald Judd wrote repeatedly about architecture. He converted existing buildings. He made sketches for projects, some of which were realised by architects. He designed furniture that was manufactured in series. And he made his position clear in exhibitions, for instance in the form of the installation *Stage Set*, which he designed for the Austrian Museum of Applied Arts in Vienna in 1991.[26]

Judd's position in the 1980s must have greatly suited many architects, above all in Europe, who wanted to liberate themselves from the stylistic confines of postmodernist architecture. Every indication of a supposed relationship between Minimal Art and architecture was therefore extremely welcome. For example the frequently quoted statement by Tony Smith, who on account of his career as an architect is often seen as a guarantor of Minimal Art's closeness to architecture, sound almost like a founding myth. Smith had early steel sculptures such as *Die* (1962) made by specialists. He recalls that he often ordered them by telephone without even making a drawing.[27] The vocabulary of architecture was deliberately transferred to visual art. For example *Scale Models and Drawings* was an exhibition held in early 1967 in the Dwan Gallery in New York. Other artists also supported the notion that Minimal Art developed from the spirit of architecture. Robert Smithson emphasised that his early sculptures were made under the impressions he had gained from collaborating with an architectural firm on an airport project in 1966. Sol LeWitt learned how to use plan sketches, grids and diagrams while he was a graphic artist in I.M. Pei's office in 1955–56 and, as he said began to understand the process from the idea to the result.[28] As soon as they had the necessary means the artist delegated the production of large-scale works to assistants and specialists. Judd took the help of engineers when he had to estimate how much a sheet of aluminium would deflect. Sol LeWitt still has his *Wall Drawings* made by assistants. Towards the end of the 1960s "nonstudio" or "post-studio production" became a matter of course.[29]

But does the delegation of the production process represent a valid argument for asserting that a practice is architectural? Was the point not also, or perhaps even primarily, to meet the rapidly growing demand for large-scale sculptures in the course of the 1960s? It is a fact that museums and collectors greeted the possibility of having large format sculptures made locally by local technicians as this eliminated transport costs. And, not least importantly, by delegating production the artists were able to satisfy the increasing appetite of the art world for large sculptures.

It is clear that the sheer size of the art works, or the artefacts as it was liked to call them in order to indicate the departure from tradition in terms of language also, moves these in the proximity of architecture. The first artist whom the critic Gregory Battcock mentions in the introduction to *Minimal Art, A Critical Anthology* is the Mexican sculptor-architect Mathias Goeritz. His gigantic structures such as the *Torres de la Ciudad Satelite* (1957) in Mexico City erected with Luis Barragan, do indeed appear to anticipate Minimal Art. One of the icons of Minimal Art is the photograph of Bladen's sculpture *X*. Like Samson it braces itself between the columns of the sculpture hall engaging in combat with the mighty architectural structure. *X* was the main attraction of the exhibition *Scale as Content*, held in 1967 in the Corcoran Gallery of Art in Washington, D.C., and the title is programmatic for the new dimensions of sculpture. The photograph, which does not reveal that the work is a wooden construction, suggests that the minimalist sculpture breaks out of the architectural confines (while at the same time taking them as its starting point) and so to speak gives the starting shot for the large-scale sculptures by Kenneth Snelson and Robert Grosvenor, and indeed for the site-specific sculptures by Richard Serra or the earthworks by Robert Smithson and Michael Heizer.

Once again the architect convert to art Tony Smith appears to offer "proof" of the architectural roots of Minimal Art. In an interview he recalls a nighttime drive at the beginning of the 1950s along the uncompleted New Jersey Turnpike, which brought him past industrial landscapes:

> "The road and much of the landscape was artificial, and yet it couldn't be called a work of art. On the other hand, it did something for me that art had never done. At first I didn't know what it was, but its effect was to liberate me from many of the views I had had about art. It seemed that there had been a reality there that had not had any expression in art ... There is no way you can frame it, you just have to experience it."[30]

Essentially this passage deals with Smith's fascination with the sublime. In his case his aesthetic feelings are stimulated by an industrial landscape rather than a mountain one. But the quotation also indicates the limited effect of the artwork when compared to the effect produced by real, built landscapes. It is therefore not so much proof of a connection between architecture and art as an indication of a theme that art would like to depict or new territory it would like to occupy and therefore I read Smiths' statement as an indication of Minimal Art's urge to expand. It is from this perspective also that I view the interest of the 1960s artists in spatial-temporal processes. *Passages in Modern Sculpture* was the title Rosalind Krauss gave her influential book that appeared in 1977 and that presents the history of sculpture from the viewpoint of Minimal Art. The new sculpture allowed one to see the

Ronald Bladen, *X*, installed in *Scale as Content*, Corcoran Gallery of Art, Washington, D.C. 1967.

Carl Andre, one-person exhibition, Tibor de Nagy Gallery, New York, 1965, with *Crib*, 1965, *Compound*, 1965, and *Coin*, 1965.

surroundings in a new light. The critic Michael Benedikt wrote in 1966 regarding the sculptures by Robert Morris and Donald Judd in the exhibition *Ten* in the Virginia Dwan Gallery in New York:

> "The Morris ... threw a particular weight of interest on the gallery boundaries, especially the walls, which it closely resembled. Although grayish, the row of six waist-high galvanized iron boxes by Judd also seemed to sculpt space outward, throwing as much interest on the space around it as it attracted to itself. In both cases one felt as if one were strolling around inside an important aspect of the work."[31]

A number of minimalist sculptures were even made for specific sites. After the weight of Carl Andre's sculpture *Well* in the group exhibition *Shape and Structure* in the Tibor de Nagy Gallery in New York 1964 threatened to cause the floor to collapse the artist dismounted the beams and laid them out anew under the title *Redan*, in order to better distribute the load. For his group exhibition in the same gallery in 1965 Andre chose from the start a very light material that occupies a considerable volume namely white Styrofoam beams. Under the titles *Crib, Coin,* and *Compound* he stacked them in the gallery spaces. Robert Morris carried this initiative further in his 1970 exhibition in the Whitney Museum of American Art where he set up an almost thirty-metre-long sculpture made of hollow concrete blocks on wooden tracks. Like a weeklong performance the sculpture was set up with the help of cranes during the exhibition in front of the public and film cameras.

Monuments for the Sixties

Placing such minimalist sculptures often was (and still is) too much for many exhibition curators. Judd was so dissatisfied with the way in which his works were placed in exhibitions that he began as early as the 1970s to erect his own museum. In Marfa, Texas, he acquired over the years a considerable number of commercial and military buildings, which he converted and fitted out with furniture that he designed himself. He aim was to exhibit his own work and that of a number of colleagues under optimal conditions. His Chinati Foundation in Marfa has been since then the most important reference whenever architects think of Minimal Art. For Judd himself the place functions like the standard metre: "Somewhere a portion of contemporary art has to exist as an example of what art and its context were meant to be. Somewhere, just as the platinum-iridium meter guarantees the tape-measure, a strict measure must exists of the art of this time an place. Otherwise art is only show and monkey business."[32]

Paradoxically, towards the end of his career Donald Judd arrived again at the very position from which had he wanted to break away in his early days. That is at the European modernist ideal of the *Gesamtkunstwerk*, a utopia of art unified under the wings of architecture as embodied by the Bauhaus. Something that almost nobody—with the exception of Robert Smithson—had seen in the mid-1960s, i.e. that Minimal Art is not a radical departure from modernist values but their continuation,

Donald Judd, 15 Untitled Works in Concrete, detail, each 250 × 250 × 500 cm. Marfa, Texas 1980–84.

becomes clear in a retrospective look at Judd's practice. The massive concrete structures of Marfa function as a place to retreat to, as a bastion against the collapse of modernist values and against the threat to artistic autonomy.

The parties which Judd celebrated yearly with hundreds of friends in far-off Texas are reminiscent of apparently timeless rituals of a society complete within itself as well as of the flirt with fashion and daily life that characterises the peak period of Minimal Art. At that time the art world had enthusiastically greeted the new "look" as a something completely and utterly contemporary. The opening of the exhibition *Primary Structures* in the Jewish Museum in New York in the spring of 1966 was a lavish party. Photographs circulated in which opening guests could be seen wearing clothes that seem like minimalist artworks. In the fashion magazine *Harper's Bazaar* Judd was shown together with his wife Julie, who wore a designer dress. In other words Minimal Art was not the kind of art that distanced itself from the viewers but on the contrary both approached viewers and involved them. Its attitude to the consumer society and the American way of life was completely affirmative. Thanks to the bright shocking colours—also used at that time for cars—and the highly polished surfaces, i.e. the special "look", it readily approached what its opponents disapprovingly dismissed as "Good Design". It functioned, so to speak, as a stage and backdrop for the booming American society of the time, well matched to both the euphoria of progress and the interest in new technologies. Nothing any longer connected it to the ideology of *épater le bourgeois*, nor with the idea of art as a realm of social resistance, as an autonomous area of the social corrective. Minimal Art is more typical of the reconciliation between art and public, a public which, as the critic Brian O'Doherty remarked, was always curious about the very latest and forced the artists to frequently alter their production like car manufacturers indeed even leading them "to mimic the obsolescence of last year's Detroit models."[33] O'Doherty went as far as to assert that minimal artists pursued the goal of producing an art that promised itself longevity by satisfying the public's expectations and adapting to the requirements of the art world. In O'Doherty's words: "The capacity to adapt is, after all, the criterion for survival."[34]

It was precisely this adapting to the public, literally "moving with the times" which opponents of Minimal Art criticised. The leader of this group, critic Michael Fried, rejected Minimal Art as "theatrical", because in his opinion it was incomplete without the viewer: "Art degenerates as it approaches the condition of theatre."[35] The triumph of Minimal Art that apparently rejected the traditional categories and was poised somewhere between architecture, music and design was, he believed, a threat to art

Primary Structures Exhibition, *Frontispiece "The Primary Structures Dress"*, 1966. Photo © The Jewish Museum, New York.

as such. "The concepts of quality and value—and to the extent that these are central to art, the concept of art itself—are meaningful, or wholly meaningful, only *within* the individual arts. What lies *between* the arts is theatre."[36]

In 1967 Fried laid his finger on, or to phrase it better, tied himself up in the Gordian knot of recent art history; as mentioned above for almost forty years now attempts have been made to undo it. The minimalism knot remains tied to this day because various different interests are caught up in it and in the course of time have entangled themselves even further. Even in the mid-1960s there existed a plethora of titles for the new art: Primary Structures, Cool Art, Reductive Art, Low-Boredom Art, New Sculpture, ABC Art, Democratic Nominalism, Idiot Art, Know-Nothing Nihilism and Literalist Art were all coined within a very short space of time but ultimately the term Minimal Art gained precedence. The abundance of terms listed is an indication of the competitive struggle over the mediation of art that took place in the 1960s. Production and reception could no longer be clearly separated from one another. Artists, architects, musicians, critics, dealers and curators exerted themselves in the area of the rapidly growing art world to secure the largest possible piece of the valuable resource represented by mediation. In much the same way as the gold diggers in Alaska marked their claims critics and curators planted various stylistic terms in the fields of the art world. At the beginning of the 1970s this struggle was decided. The museum as an institution where art takes place and its value is measured has ever since then occupied the priority position in the mediation of art.

In a retrospective attempt to simplify we can identify two camps: the modernists and the post-modernists. Those whom we today describe as Modernists saw a threat to the established system of cultural values, in existence since the late nineteenth century (essence, quality, authenticity, self-referentiality within separate artistic categories, autonomy, historicity). In my view many architects still share this viewpoint although, of course, they are not opposed to Minimal Art but instead invoke it. However they invoke merely formal analogies without sharing the minimalist criticism of modernist values. That is to say they are far closer to the Judd of the 1980s than to the Judd of the 1960s. Those today described as postmodernists—in the mid-1960s the term was not yet in use—identified themselves with the new artistic values of Minimal Art (presence, look, surface, popularity, relationship to place, timelessness). For the majority of architects, i.e. the Europeans, the term postmodernism is inflammatory. In contrast to many artists, who understand this term as a specific cultural logic, architects tend to interpret it as the name for an outdated stylistic programme dating from the 1970s. Thus, according to the particular standpoint minimalism is interpreted either as a bastion against the collapse of modernist values or as a brand name for the new, either as a symbol of the American triumph or as the continuation of the European tradition. For some it is a theatre stage of a degenerate art that has prostrated itself in front of design, fashion and consumerism, for others it is quite the opposite: a guarantee that the autonomy and historicity of art are incorruptible. Therefore minimalism does not describe a historical phenomenon but is the material for an ongoing discussion, an area on which a yet-to-be-decided test of strength takes place between new and old artistic values, between American and European culture, between art and architecture.

Notes

1 "Something or nothing: Minimalism in art and architecture", Royal Academy of Arts, London, 1998, published under the title "Aspects of Minimal Architecture II", in: *Architectural Design*, 69, 5/6, May–June 1999, pp. 1–96. cf. "Aspects of Minimal Architecture I", in: *Architectural Design*, London, 1994; *Minimal Tradition, Max Bill und die "einfache" Architektur 1942–1996*, XIX Triennale die Milano, 1996, Bundesamt für Kultur (ed.) Baden, 1996.

2 Charles Jencks, "Open Discussion", in: *Architectural Design*, 69, 5/6, May–June 1999, pp. 15–17, here: p. 15.

3 Ibid., p. 16.

4 The most important references are: Gregory Battcock (ed.) *Minimal Art, A critical anthology*, New York, 1968, new edition, with an introduction by Anne Wagner, Berkeley, 1995; Rosalind Krauss, *Passages in Modern Sculpture*, New York, 1977, Frances Colpitt, *Minimal Art—A Criticial Perspective*, Ann Arbor, 1990, Gregor Stemmrich, publ., *Minimal Art, Eine kritische Retrospekive*, Dresden, 1995; James Meyer, *Minimalism, Art and Polemics in the Sixties*, New Haven, 2001.

5 Maggie Toy, "Editorial", in: *Architectural Design*, 69, 5/6, May–June 1999, p. 7.

6 Peter Murray, "Something or nothing: Minimalism in Art and Architecture", in: *Architectural Design*, 69, 5/6, May–June 1999, pp. 8–17 here: p. 8.

7 Ibid.

8 Anatxu Zabalbeascoa, Javier Rodriguez Marcos, *Minimalisms*, Barcelona, 2000; Franco Bertoni, *Architettura minimalista*, Florence, 2002.

9 Todd Gitlin, *The Sixties, Years of Hope, Days of Rage*, New York, 1987.

10 Donald Judd, "Questions to Stella and Judd, Interview by Bruce Glaser edited by Lucy R. Lippard" (1966), in: Battcock, 1968, pp. 148–164, here: p. 154.

11 Donald Judd, "Questions to Stella and Judd", in Battcock, 1968, p. 155.

12 Frank Stella, "Questions to Stella and Judd", in Battcock, 1968, 149.

13 Carl Andre, in: "Ein Interview mit Carl Andre von Phyllis Tuchman", in: Gregor Stemmrich (ed.), *Minimal Art, Eine kritische Retrospektive*, Dresden, 1995, pp. 141–161, here: p. 152.

14 Robert Morris, "Notes on Sculpture, Part 3: Notes and Non Sequiturs" (*Artforum*, vol. 5, no 10, June 1967), quoted in: *Continuous Project Altered Daily: The Writings of Robert Morris*, Cambridge, Mass., 1993, pp. 23–39, here: p. 27.

15 "Klee's way of life may have been cosmopolitan, but his art belongs to the provinces in more than one respect. Its world is a closed one—capable of being divided infinitely, but limited in its expansion. It grew by intensification, not by expansion." Clement Greenberg, "Art Chronicle: on Paul Klee (1870–1940)", in: *Partisan Review*, May–June 1941, reprinted in: Clement Greenberg, *The Collected Essays and Criticism, vol. 1, Perceptions and Judgements, 1939–1944*, edited by John O'Brian, Chicago, 1986, pp. 65–73, here: p. 66

16 Frank Stella, "Questions to Stella and Judd", in: Battcock, 1968, p. 149.

17 Ibid.

18 Morris, Ibid.

19 Donald Judd, "Questions to Stella and Judd", in Battcock, 1968, p. 154.

20 Robert Morris, "Notes on Sculpture" (1966), in: Battcock, 1968, pp. 222–235, here: p. 228.

21 Frank Stella, "Questions to Stella and Judd", in Battcock, 1968, p. 159.

22 Ibid.

23 Sol LeWitt, "The Cube" (1966), in: *Sol LeWitt*, exhibition catalogue, Museum of Modern Art, New York, 1978, p. 172.

24 Frank Stella, "Questions to Stella and Judd", in Battcock, 1968, p. 158.

25 "Aspects of Minimal Architecture", in: *Architectural Design*, 64, no 7/8, July–August 1994, pp. 1–96, here: p. 8–9.

26 Cf. *Donald Judd, Architektur*, exhibition catalogue, Österreichisches Museum für angewandte Kunst, Vienna, 1991.

27 Cf. Joan H. Pachner, "Tony Smith – Von der Architektur zur Skulptur", in: *Tony Smith, Skulpturen 1961–1969*, exhibition catalogue, Westfälisches Landesmuseum Münster, 1988, pp. 49–71, here: p. 59.

28 Cf. Trevor Fairbrother, "Sol LeWitt's drawings and the art of 'logical statement'", in: *Sol LeWitt Drawings 1958–1992*, exhibition catalogue, Haags Gemeentemuseum, 1992, n.p.

29 Cf. the chapter "Process issues", in: Frances Colpitt, *Minimal Art, The Critical Retrospective*, Seattle, 1990, pp. 7–39.

30 Tony Smith, quoted in Michael Fried, "Art and Objecthood" (1967), in: Battcock, 1968, pp. 116–147, here: p. 131.

31 Michael Benedikt, "Sculpture as architecture: New York letter, 1966–67", in: Battcock, 1968, pp. 61–91, here: p. 74.

32 Donald Judd, *Complete Writings 1975–1986*, Eindhoven, 1987, p. 111. Quoted in Brigitte Huck, "Donald Judd: Architekt", in: *Donald Judd, Architektur*, Österreichisches Museum für angewandte Kunst, 1991, pp. 17–21, here: p. 18.

33 Brian O'Doherty, "Minus Plato", in: Battcock, 1968, pp. 251–255, here: p. 251.

34 Ibid., p. 252.

35 Michael Fried, "Art and Objecthood", in Battcock, 1968, p. 141.

36 Ibid., p. 142.

Essential, Meta-, Trans-. The Chimeras of Minimalist Architecture

Ilka & Andreas Ruby

The term minimalist architecture is itself a paradox. On the one hand its meaning seems entirely clear, on hearing its name there springs to mind a definite image of a particular kind of architecture yet, on the other hand, the harder you try to grasp it, the more the subject avoids definition. Instead of a clearly outlined concept we are faced with a soft mass that resists any attempts at fixing it down because it compliantly changes shape to suit each effort at defining it. Minimalist architecture is ultimately whatever you want it to be.

The malleable nature of the term has certainly to do with the fact that it has never been properly defined. In contrast to many other such -isms we cannot identify a single founding act of minimalist architecture. There exists no manifesto by its protagonists (comparable, say, to the manifesto on the founding of the Bauhaus in 1919) nor was there ever an exhibition that served as the media initiation of a new style (such as the exhibition *International Style* in 1934 in the Museum of Modern Art in New York). It appears that minimalist architecture has always been ahead of its discourse, which explains why the term never had to be defined but could be taken for granted. The historical pre-existence of Minimal Art allowed minimalist architecture to fabricate an identity of its own by using a technique of implicit reference without ever positioning or exposing itself in the course of doing so. In a certain sense minimalist architecture used Minimal Art as a nominal reference space by means of which every kind of architecture that, in some way or other, recalled the look of Minimal Art was automatically declared minimalist architecture.[1] As a consequence, over the past 15 years, a group of architects has grown up whose work we wish to describe here as "Essential Minimal" as it represents the core of what today is generally associated with the term minimalist architecture.

I. Essential Minimalism

Like each tendency this movement is not homogeneous but is made up of a number of sub-tendencies. These include "London Minimal", defined by the cool elegance and controlled understatement of John Pawson (for many the personal reincarnation of minimalism in architecture) and which includes architects such as Tony Fretton, David Chipperfield or David Adjaye; the "Mediterranean Minimal ", represented by Claudio Silvestrin, Alberto Campo Baeza, Edouardo Souto de Moura, who fuel the

John Pawson, Pawson House, London 1999.

Edouardo Souto de Moura, Bom Jesus House, Braga, Portugal 1989–94. View of Roof.

movement with strictly calculated injections that seem above all to invoke the beauty of the Mediterranean landscape; "Swiss Minimal", in which the tradition of high-quality Swiss manufacturing is incorporated in architecture (Diener & Diener, Meili + Peter, Gigon/Guyer among others.)

Outside these groups there exists a series of charismatic individualists each of whom, in a certain respect, represents a tendency of their own: Tadao Ando, who made the smoothness of his concrete into a personal trade mark—incidentally in the early 1980s, i.e. before the emergence of architectural minimalism, Peter Zumthor, who uses a craftsman's approach to materials to breathe new life into the aura of vanished times and regions and is frequently cited as a figurehead of minimalism while himself denying any association with the movement and, finally, Herzog & de Meuron, who with their ambivalent manipulations of images, material and typologies take a somewhat antagonistic approach to their minimalist colleagues and consequently can be included in this category only with considerable reservations.

What holds these various sub-tendencies together is a collective "look" that can be described in terms of a number of design preferences: introversion, simple geometry, smooth surfaces, absence of visible details and "authenticity" of materials. Basically it is this collective look that forms the media image of Essential Minimalism as a unified and homogeneous tendency in architecture. However, this image conceals the fact that the protagonists frequently employ the shared design vocabulary for very different purposes and reasons. This difference between the motivations is one of the principal reasons why it is so problematic to use the term minimalism in any context other than its apparent self-evidence. Therefore, if we wish to usefully employ the term in the discussion of architecture it is essential to first examine these various motivations.

1. Objectifying Architecture

For the architecture of German-speaking Switzerland, which represents a significant sector of Essential Minimalism, the relationship to Minimal Art was doubtless a welcome means of positioning itself in the prevailing situation of architecture in the 1980s.[2] In terms of styles this epoch was, we know, dominated by Postmodernism and Deconstructivism, two tendencies to which Swiss-German minimalists such as Peter Märkli, Diener & Diener, Meili & Peter, to mention just a few, maintained a clear distance. The eclectic excitement of postmodern style collages was as suspect to them as the formal complexity and theoretical bias of Deconstructivism. They counteracted the conceptual "external" referencing of architecture, i.e. the referral to systems "foreign" to architecture, with an introspection based on "intrinsically architectural" values. Instead of approaching architecture using philosophical and linguistic processes or those adapted from the natural sciences as for example Peter Eisenman—the intellectual

Gigon/Guyer, Kirchner-Museum, Davos, Switzerland 1998–92. View toward Entrance.

precursor of deconstructivist architecture, the Swiss minimalists were interested in a new "self-presentation" of architecture. The principle of reduction here served as a means of "defending the truth and the delight of seeing against the propaganda of form in utterly confused cultural circumstances" as Marcel Meili put it.[3]

To keep the upper hand in this culture conflict the German-Swiss architects developed a radical reduction that outstripped even Mies' understanding of "less is more". Whereas Mies van der Rohe reduced architecture's envelope in order to reveal its structural logic they make the building's structure disappear in the interior of a closed block. The building ceases to be a building in order to become entirely an object that presents neither its function nor its construction but solely an intellectualised idea of order that holds up a corrective mirror to the chaotic condition of its surroundings.

2. The Essence of Memory

The belief in a concentrated essence of architecture, which is clearly distinguishable from everything that is not architecture, also lies at the basis of Peter Zumthor's work. "I believe that architecture today needs to reflect on the tasks and possibilities which are inherently its own. Architecture is not a vehicle or a symbol for things that do not belong to its essence. In a society which celebrates the inessential, architecture can put up a resistance, counteract the waste of forms and meanings, and speak its own language."[4] Yet Zumthor occupies a special place among the representatives of Swiss Minimalism. What seems to be "minimalist" about his work is ultimately the expression of a profoundly metaphysical culture of remembering places and subjects. Zumthor sees each of his buildings as an "envelope and background for life which goes on in and around it."[5] The meaning of the emptiness they produce lies in the way they allow the subject a quasi-spiritual experience of himself. "Our perceptive faculties grow quiet, unprejudiced and unacquisitive. They reach beyond signs and symbols, they are open, empty. It is as if we could see something on which we cannot focus our consciousness. Here, in this perceptual vacuum, a memory may surface, a memory which seems to issue from the depths of time."[6] Furthermore, for Zumthor memory is also the decisive condition for the unity between architecture and place which he aims at: "I believe that buildings which become gradually accepted into their surroundings must have the ability to appeal to our emotions and minds in various ways. But since our feelings and understanding are rooted in the past, our sensuous connections with a building must respect the process of remembering."[7]

Morger & Degelo, Haus Müller, Staufen, Switzerland 1998–99. Exposed Corner.

Peter Zumthor, Thermalbad Vals, Vals, Switzerland 1996. Interior pool.

The material is one of the decisive catalysts in this process of remembering. For instance in his Residential Home for the Elderly, Masans in Chur, Switzerland (1993) Zumthor very consciously uses materials that remind residents of the home of their earlier life in the surrounding villages: larch wood and tufa stone. The intention is that these materials should make it easier for them to feel at home in this new place.

In his Thermalbad Vals, Switzerland (1996) Zumthor clads the underground baths with gneiss quarried from 1,000 metres away in the mountain. The recourse to nature could not be clearer: the baths are made of the same stone as the mountain in which they are embedded and from which the warm water, in which one takes healing baths, springs. For Zumthor the baths are a medium that can bring people in contact with the essential core of their existence. Unlike the profane baths of the Dutch Centerparks, they are not a place for solely having fun but serve primarily the cleansing of both body and spirit.

3. Cleansing by Introverting

This interest in "cleansing" contemporary culture of its hybrids and contaminations represents a constant rhetorical topos of Essential Minimalism. The product designer Massimo Vignelli sees in minimalism not a style "but a far-reaching reaction to the noise, the visual noise the disorder and the vulgarity"[8] of our times. Seen from this viewpoint the ostentatious purity and cleanliness of minimalist architecture is not a purist aestheticism but part of a perceptual therapy that treats the subject shattered by post-modernism. Minimalist architecture according to Maggie Toy, allows those living in it: "To free themselves from the everyday clutter of life and to relax in a calm haven of elegant simplicity devoid of fuss and clutter, soothed by the tranquillity and restfulness of unencumbered space."[9]

There is something bizarre about this therapeutic viewpoint and yet it seems to explain, with blinding clarity, one of the primary characteristics of Essential Minimalism—the extrovert introversion of the building. The building's almost hermetic seclusion from the outside has, looked at from this therapeutic angle, the function of the Virgin's protective mantle—as depicted in numerous Marian images—that shields us from the dangers of external reality. The interior of the building becomes a time-out of reality in which a lost order of things is offered a last asylum.

This kind of architectural reality management is applied with a canonical clarity in Alberto Campo Baeza's Centro Baléar de Innovación Tecnologica in Inca, Majorca, Spain (1999). Instead of exposing the requisite office spaces to the soulless reality of a business park in Majorca, Baeza enclosed the triangular site with a continuous boundary wall that effectively makes the surroundings vanish. The offices are located in completely glazed pavilions from which you can look either into the "secret

Alberto Campo Baeza, Centro Baléar de Innovación Tecnologica, Inca, Mallorca, Spain 1999. "Secret Garden" with offices on the left and boundary wall on the right.

garden" at the centre of the courtyard or at the continuous boundary wall. The world outside exists only as the excluded other of this enclosure. As a purely outside place it is of no interest to Campo Baeza's interior world, nor is the question how this world is perceived from outside—which explains why the project is always published without any photographs of the exterior.

The elimination of the outside is a familiar motif in Tadao Ando's urban single-family houses from the 1970s and '80s which he used to formulate a critique of the heterogeneous urbanity of Japanese cities: "The dullness of our environment reveals how senseless it is to abandon and submerge the self in its surroundings."[10] For Ando the only possible way to behave in such a context is to negate it entirely, he views enclosure with windowless concrete walls as the only means of giving the individual space in which to develop. These spaces are, as a rule, lit from within, from an outdoor space integrated in the house. This space is still climatically connected to the outside but otherwise completely conditioned by the interior space of the house.

To the outside, Ando's houses appear to have an effect similar to that created by minimalist sculptures. Just as the roaming gaze of the viewer finds no detail it can rest upon in the smooth surfaces of objects by Donald Judd, Robert Morris and Tony Smith and therefore almost compulsively ends up examining the architectural features of the gallery space, our gaze glances off the bare concrete facades of Ando's town houses beginning instead to develop an interest in the irregular structures of the neighbouring buildings. However, this dialectic activating of external urban space caused by the building's abstraction is like an accidental side effect. Essentially Ando follows the classical Japanese tradition of opening the house onto the landscape, and he does this wherever the context offers a landscape of a particular quality, for example in his Church on the Water in Hokkaidō, Japan (1988). If the site cannot offer this quality then Ando closes his building off from its surroundings and compensates for the lack of a relationship to the outside by creating an "implanted" outdoor space.[11]

4. Reduction as a Criticism of Consumerism

As well as rejecting the contemporary city the internal emigration of Ando's architecture represents a moral critique of late capitalist society. Ando sees the continual stimulation of desires as a serious threat to the subject: "Once a desire approaches perfection, it grows larger and stimulates other ambitions. Man enters a never-ending cycle and becomes dominated by his own excessive desires," writes Tadao Ando. An architecture based on reduction could help people discover their true essential

Tadao Ando, Row House Sumiyoshi, Japan 1975–76. Street facade and interior courtyard.

Tadao Ando, Church on the Water, Hokkaido, Japan 1988. View from the Nave toward the Cross.

desires: "Simplification through the elimination of all surface decorations, the employment of minimal, symmetrical compositions and limited materials constitutes a challenge to contemporary civilisation."[12]

John Pawson also sees his reductionist architecture as a critical corrective to western consumerism. Whereas in the nineteenth century a comfortably furnished house did not have more than a few hundred objects, "Nowadays we are drowning in possessions."[13] In order to uncover the buried meaning of our existence Pawson refers to the moral integrity of aesthetic reduction as embodied in the Japanese notion of "wabi" (voluntary poverty). As an architectural reference Pawson cites the architecture of the Shakers—a religious community based on Quakerism which voluntarily embraced a life conducted in poverty, sexual abstinence and the avoidance of contact with society and also forbade decoration and ornament—as well as the architecture of the Cistercians.

Interestingly Pawson achieved international fame above all through his boutiques for the American fashion designer Calvin Klein: Tokyo 1994, New York 1995, Seoul 1996, Hamburg 1999, Paris 1999, Dubai 1999, Taipei 2000—the speed with which the shops he designed sprouted out of the ground in various world capitals does indeed bear a certain similarity to the feverish burst of colonization in which the reformed Christian religious order once erected its monasteries across the heathen world of eastern Europe. And indeed Pawson's description of Cistercian architecture in which "ornament and decoration were viewed as superfluous luxury that would only distract the worshippers from the adoration of God," could be equally well applied to his Calvin Klein boutiques—albeit with a little switch as regards the object of adoration.

For Pawson's former office partner, Claudio Silvestrin, the unornamented architecture of the Cistercians also forms one of the major sources of inspiration for his work where, according to his own words, his main interest lies in: "Questioning the conventional aspects of consumerism."[14] To fully understand the deeper significance of this statement one must realise that, since 1999, Silvestrin has been responsible for the "world architectural image" of Giorgio Armani and in this function has designed the Armani boutiques in Paris, Milan, Düsseldorf, Florence, Moscow, Naples, Boston, Chicago, Tokyo, Sao Paolo, Seoul, Athens, Atlanta, Zurich, Vienna, Rome, Peking and Hong Kong.

Thus an aesthetic of renunciation, practiced by a monastic order many of whose members, as a result of their relentlessly ascetic life, did not live beyond the age of 25 was smoothly reapplied to the luxury consumer culture of a lifestyle community whose adherents (not much older than 25) sought inspiration on how to spend their surplus wealth. This fascinating phenomenon became possible as a result of a transformation of consumer culture that occurred during the 1990s in which the focus of interest moved from the products themselves to the values attributed to them. The brand acquired meaning as a space of reference in which these values were anchored. The increasing

John Pawson, Calvin Klein Store, New York 1995.
View of shop interior from upper gallery.

spread of this brand name culture made it necessary for exclusive designer labels to distance themselves from the mainstream. Minimalism turned out to be doubly suited as a means of achieving this clear distinction, because its aesthetic of emptiness initially attracts the gaze of passers-by and, as the naked walls offer no further distraction, attracts them magnetically to the strategically placed goods. This uncommonly effective display system made minimalism the dominant tendency in retail store design in the 1990s.

However, it only became the leading design paradigm of the urban professionals as a result of the decision by Canadian journalist Tyler Brulé, to use minimalism as the atmospheric leitmotiv of his lifestyle magazine *Wallpaper**, founded in 1997. Adopting the figure-ground scheme of the minimalist presentation of goods, Brulé staged photo shootings of trendy models in the latest designer fashions against an atmospheric background of minimalist architecture.[15] As the boundaries between advertising and editorial content in the graphic layout of *Wallpaper** are deliberately blurred in order to make visual consumption a total experience, the architecture often emerges out of its passive background role and itself becomes a product. In the process the meaning of the architecture changes decisively due to the presence of people in the photographed space (an effect that architecture photographs of the same projects always take pains to avoid but that was, in contrast, emphatically demanded by the artists who produced Minimal Art). This animation with human beings means that the spiritual, esoteric quality is unintentionally switched into a completely profane, everyday culture, translating minimalism from an architectural style into a lifestyle.

II. Meta-Minimal

So the meaning of minimalist architecture changed into practically its opposite. Thanks to its success it became the incarnation of precisely that superficial, materialist culture it had always seen itself as a critical alternative to. The fact that this development did not lead to a conflict of conscience for, of all people, Herzog & de Meuron suggests that they are not so much the model example of minimalist architecture as which they are often regarded but in fact its *enfant terrible*. In contrast to its professed representatives their handling of minimalism in architecture is of a decisively strategic nature. Essentially they used it as a label for the development of their own branding when, at the end of the 1980s, they were seeking to stake their claim in the international architectural landscape.[16] On this account only a limited number of their projects can be ascribed to Essential Minimalism. These include, for example, the Stone House in Tavole, Italy (1988), the Goetz Collection in Munich (1992) and the Anti-

Herzog & de Meuron, Antipodes I, Student Housing for the Université de Bourgogne, Dijon, France, 1990–92. View of campus with student hostels connected by covered walkways.

Herzog & de Meuron, Eberswalde Technical School Library, Eberswalde, Germany 1994–99. Street facade with printed concrete and glass panels.

podes Student Hostel in Dijon, France (1992). Even though, at places, other motifs already announce their emergence in these projects, they still remain within the boundaries of Swiss Essential Minimal (a simple geometric box with flush surfaces, barely visible details and a few, decisive materials). But from the mid-1990s Herzog & de Meuron begin to increasingly overlay the classical minimalist agenda with other interests. These are, in particular, the decontextualisation of the material and the introduction of the image as a medium of architectural information. The projects resulting from this research on the one hand explode established notions of minimalist architecture while on the other frequently seem like a feedback to earlier Herzog & de Meuron projects, yet in some way altered. For example: the horizontal bands of fibre cement panels in the Ricola Storage Building in Laufen, Switzerland (1996) reoccur in the form of the copper bands wrapped around the Signal Box, Auf dem Wolf in Basel, Switzerland (1992), the rubble stone facade of the Stone House, which could be read as a reference to traditional building methods in the region, is resurrected in the Dominus Winery in Yountville, California, USA (1996–98), but this time in the shape of stone-filled baskets normally used to prevent the erosion of embankments. In precisely the same way the Eberswalde Technical School Library in Germany (1996) refers back to the Goetz Collection building as well as to the Antipodes Student Housing but with the difference that the more recent building tattoos the naked minimal box over and over with images directly incised into both the concrete and the glass by means of a new technique.

Through this strategy of continually pushing out the boundaries (numerous other examples could be cited) Herzog & de Meuron moved architectural minimalism into its self-reflective phase, so to speak. They appeared to be saying: now that the vocabulary has been defined we can begin to play with it instead of just rattling off the canon. By broadening the definition they have created a situation in which many architects, previously never associated with minimalism, could employ its vocabulary even though they followed completely different goals.

For example an architect such as Dominique Perrault could only very loosely be described as a minimalist. After all, the major ambition behind his work is to make architecture disappear whereas minimalist architecture, as explained above, tends to strengthen the building's presence by emphasising its qualities as an object. Where the local situation allowed Perrault to realise his aim by creating an artificial topography of earth mounds and lowering his building among them thus making it invisible. In the projects presented in this book this strategy was not viable so, in order nevertheless to use his conjuring trick, Perrault interestingly turns to a minimalist, object-centred architecture: closed boxes that reflect the gaze by means of mirrored or opaque facades and in this way make the building indirectly invisible.

Equally, it would certainly also be an exaggeration to accuse Rem Koolhaas of having converted to minimalism. Nevertheless, in his Guggenheim Eremitage in Las Vegas, Nevada (1999) he employs a clearly minimalist vocabulary. The answer to the puzzle is not hard to find. Most probably the minimalist

Herzog & de Meuron, Stone House, Tavole, Italy 1982–88. Main view with exposed concrete structure framing the terrace.

Herzog & de Meuron, Dominus Winery, Yountville, California, 1995–98. Facade made of stone-filled gabions.

box seemed to Koolhaas the instrument best suited to placing this branch of the St. Petersburg gallery in the centre of Las Vegas' largest and most surreal casino in such a way that the perception of the exhibition is not impaired by the surroundings. Even in the explanation for his choice of materials the convinced "dirty realist" Koolhaas adheres to the minimalist "must" of authentic materials: whereas the casino is resplendent in fake marble and Styrofoam ornament the CorTen steel on the walls of his gallery does not pretend to be anything other than what it is.[17]

III. Trans-Minimal

Analogous to the cases of Perrault and Koolhaas there are numerous similar examples in the current production of architecture that indicate the existence of a Meta-Minimalism (a number of them are presented in this book).

The meta-minimalist transformation and decontextualisation of minimalist architectural effects makes minimalist architecture—which is itself already diffuse and multi-directional—diffuse even further, thereby incurring the risk of dissolving altogether. Thus Meta-Minimalism exposes a new view of minimalist architecture in which it is not the "return to the essential" that appears to typify such architecture but, on the contrary, its striking ability to expand into other contexts (the excursion referred to above into the world of luxury consumerism is only one example among many). On the other hand minimalist architecture has continually failed in its attempts to refer back to its nominal and historical essence, Minimal Art. The assertion that the architectural use of formal design principles derived from Minimal Art could establish continuity between Minimal Art and minimal architecture is one of the most frequently cultivated misunderstandings of Essential Minimalism. The reason for this discrepancy lies in the fact that minimalist artists never used these design principles for their own sake but as a means towards achieving a specific end. At the centre of their artistic activity is the discovery of a new "inclusive" space that they wish to create by dissolving the boundaries around the artwork and allowing it expand into the space surrounding it. In contrast the architects of Essential Minimal have no interest in this "goal", their sole interest is in the design means which minimal artists developed to achieve this aim, i.e. taking the sculpture off its pedestal, eliminating composition, smooth surfaces, primary geometry, etc. which the architects (mis)understood, in the sense of "less is more", as a continuation of the reductionist aesthetic of modern architecture.[18]

OMA Office for Metropolitan Architecture, Guggenheim Hermitage, Las Vegas, Nevada USA 1999. Exterior Wall of Gallery as inserted in the building envelope of The Venetian.

Dominique Perrault, Olympic Velodrome and Swimming Pool, Berlin 1992–97. Building volume embedded in the mounted earth socle.

Paradoxically, the use of these design principles in architecture led to precisely the opposite of what minimalist artists aimed at: that is, it did not dissolve boundaries but renewed and heightened the distinction between the object and its surroundings. The border between inside and outside is not abolished but maximised. The most significant reason for this reverse effect probably lies in the fact that, in appropriating Minimal Art, the architects unthinkingly applied their own ideas of inside and outside, of object and space to art. In the process they overlooked the fact that, in Minimal Art, the expansion of the artwork into the space surrounding it is possible only because the artworks have no interior space. The immaculate surfaces of their closed elements throw the gaze back into the space of the viewer. The apparent reduction of Donald Judd's wall boxes or the floor sculptures of Carl Andre activate the surrounding space in which they are exhibited (or to put it better, which they enact). This space—which in the architectural interpretation of Minimal Art transforms into external space—is for the artwork the primary sphere of its social experience. Yet as buildings, in contrast to artworks, do have an interior space that, in the utilitarian sense, also represents their *raison d'être*, the primary social experience of architecture includes both the surrounding space (=outside) and their internal space. That very expansion of the art object into its surrounding space achieved by Minimal Art cannot, in an architecture with similar ambitions, be restricted to the outside of the building but must also work inwards, towards the interior. Therefore the operative logic of minimalist art (the reflection of external space on the surface of the object) must, in an architecture in sympathy with such art, transform into a transition of the architectural boundary between external and internal space. In order to establish this transitional quality it is highly likely that architecture must depart from the formal canon it extracted from Minimal Art and instead search for architectural processes suited to achieving this aim.

Instead of cladding the building with opaque or translucent materials—the minimalist transparency phobia being fairly obvious—it would then be important to make the facades more visually permeable. The "aura potential" of minimalist architecture would, as a consequence, no longer be limited to producing fetish interiors but could finally extend its effect outwards into external space.[19]

Instead of using the symbolic order of "simple geometric forms" to separate the building from its surroundings (which, of necessity, are always derogatorily referred to as chaotic) architecture could introduce more complex geometries that would allow the development of a topographical continuity between inside and outside.[20]

The pseudo-romantic restriction to "natural" and "authentic" materials could be replaced by a contemporary understanding of materials that is based on the nature of everyday reality (and which

Herzog & de Meuron, Prada Tokyo Shop and Offices, Tokyo 2000–03 (design). Montage of the Building's Exterior.

would, of course, include synthetic materials). The material selected by architecture would then no longer appear as an idealised antithesis to the supposed perversions of reality but would be revealed as a medium that gives the materiality of the context a heightened presence.[21]

A minimalist architecture that positions itself as a conceptual continuation of Minimal Art would, by definition, be an architecture that transcends its boundaries, no matter whether these boundaries are set by architecture itself or by others. Minimalism in architecture would therefore always ultimately flow into maximalism.

Notes

1 In this context see in particular the theme issues of various architecture magazines: *Rassegna*, 36/4 [Minimal]; *Lotus International*, 81, 1994 [Neominimalismo]; *Architectural Design* 7/8, 1994 [Aspects of Minimal Architecture]; Techniques & Architecture 423, 1996 [Tendance Minimale]; *Architectural Design* 5/6, 1999 [Aspects of Minimal Architecture II]. See also: Josep Maria Montaner, "Minimalismos", *El Croquis*, 62/63, 1993; Anatxu Zabalbeascoa, Javier Rodriguez Marcos, *Minimalisms*, Barcelona 2000; and finally Franco Bertoni, *Minimalistische Architektur*, Basel 2002.

2 On the relationship between Swiss-German architecture and Minimal Art see the enlightening text by Hans Frei, "Leave the Channels—follow the Roots", *Arch+* 129/130, December 1995, pp. 103–106.

3 Marcel Meili, quoted in Hans Frei, 1995, p. 103.

4 Peter Zumthor, "A Way of Looking at Things", in: *a+u*, February 1998 [Extra Edition Peter Zumthor], p. 24.

5 Peter Zumthor, 1998. p. 10.

6 Peter Zumthor, 1998, p. 14.

7 Peter Zumthor, 1998, p. 16.

8 Massimo Vignelli, quoted in Franco Bertoni, 2002, p. 57.

9 Maggie Toy, "Editorial", in: *Architectural Design*, 5/6, 1999 [Aspects of Minimal Architecture II], p. 7.

10 Tadao Ando, "A Wedge in Circumstances", in: *Tadao Ando. Complete Works*, edited by Francesco Dal Co, London 1995, p. 444.

11 On this account Koji Taki sees Ando's architecture not as Minimalism, but as the expression of a "monotonality", that Ando derives from the inheritance of traditional Japanese architecture. Koji Taki, *Minimalism or Monotonality? A Contextual Analysis of Tadao Ando's Method*, New York 1984.

12 Tadao Ando, "Interior, Exterior", in: *Tadao Ando. Complete Works*, 1995, p. 449.

13 John Pawson, *Minimal*, London 1998, p. 12.

14 Claudio Silvestrin, in: Franco Bertoni, *Claudio Silvestrin*, Florence 1999, p. 165.

15 For example Peter Zumthor's thermal baths in Vals, *Wallpaper** 8, 1997, pp. 204–05. On the cultural function of minimalist architecture in the event-based economy of shopping and the museum world see Dietmar Steiner, "Promotional Architecture", *Architectural Design* [Fashion and Architecture], 6, 2000, pp. 20–23.

16 Until the mid-1980s the architecture of Herzog & de Meuron was not yet characterised by the minimalists' monolithic understanding of form but by a more articulated formal language that Jacques Herzog traces back to their early models, Hans Scharoun and Alvar Aalto. See: Jeffrey Kipnis, "A Conversation with Jacques Herzog", in: *El Croquis* 60 + 84 [Herzog & de Meuron 1981–2000], p. 36.

17 Rem Koolhaas, in an unpublished lecture given at the symposium "Trans-Urbanism", NAi Rotterdam, 29 November 2001.

18 For a significant example see: *Less is more. Minimalism in Architecture and the other Arts*, ed. by Vittorio E. Savi , Josep M. Montaner. [Catalogue of the same name produced for the UIA Congress Barcelona 1996]

19 See here the projects by Shigeru Ban in this book.

20 An ambition that is decisive for, above all, infrastructuralism and the architecture of topological landscapes. Zaha Hadid did important preliminary work here, from the late-1980s dissolving the opposition between figure and ground (the building and the space surrounding it) in a "tectonic landscape". Rem Koolhaas' Bibliothèques de Jussieu (Paris, 1993) forms, finally, the starting point of the architecture of the continuous surface that has reached its interim highpoint with FOA's Yokohama Terminal (Yokohama, 2002).

21 On this point see the projects by R&Sie... in this book, likewise Blur at the Swiss National Exhibition *Expo.02* by Diller + Scofidio (Yverdon-les-Bains, 2002).

Projects I The buildings and projects in this book are presented in three chapters, which we have entitled "Essential Minimalism", "Meta-Minimalism" and "Trans-Minimalism". These headings suggest that, instead of dealing with the notion of minimalism in architecture in a canonical fashion, the intention here is to show how this contemporary international movement moves towards its future by employing strategies that are new and quite often surprising.

The chapter on Essential Minimalism in this book deals most closely with the forms and the look we tend to expect from a minimalist architecture. Its basic criteria are derived from American Minimal Art of the 1960s: the use of simple geometric forms, the modular principle, addition rather than composition, the rejection of spatial hierarchies – including the frame and the plinth – and surfaces with a smooth industrial appearance that negate any character of hand-made individuality. Despite the apparent simplicity of these works the effect they make is extremely complex. This applies both to sculpture and to the space in which it stands, which forms part of the concept and with which it engages in an exciting relationship.

In accordance with our definition minimalist architecture should also be characterised by these criteria and by a corresponding complexity – simplicity or reduction do not necessarily have anything to do with minimalism. In this chapter Essential Minimalism's starting point is located in Japan. A presentation of a number of important positions, primarily in Swiss and Austrian architecture, follows. Essential Minimalism is frequently distinguished by qualities of introspection and introversion; it transforms the building into an object with a perfected external form and surfaces, which reveal nothing about its construction or function. Only a few buildings in this category correspond with the external world by employing strategies of translucence or transparency. Generally the architectural object draws a clear line between itself and its—often heterogeneous—surroundings and represents the standpoint that "least is most" which can be read on the one hand as an attempt at imposing self-restraint and order and on the other as a criticism of the surrounding architecture, the city and, ultimately, of the social conditions. At the same time the style's particular elegance has effected an inversion of these values: Essential Minimalism has, not without a certain irony, proved a most suitable architectural formula for particularly prestigious commissions in the public, business and private sectors.

Angeli Sachs

Tadao Ando

Tadao Ando was one of the first to enter the field of architectural minimalism where he occupies a highly individual and complex position. To put it the other way around one could also say that he is one of the most influential models for the representatives of Essential Minimalism.

Many of his buildings, above all the earlier ones, are characterised by simplicity and introversion and by the use of fair-faced concrete both externally and internally which, in terms of craftsmanship, is so well made that it has a smooth almost silky texture. As William J. R. Curtis remarks: "Simplification sometimes results in the simplistic, but with Ando it leads to concentration." As a result Ando's buildings are places of spatial intensity and calm in often-heterogeneous surroundings.

This is particularly true of his Azuma House in Sumiyoshi dating from1975–76, which Ando describes as the starting point for his subsequent works. This closed concrete box in central Osaka, inserted in a timber-built terraced housing development dating from the pre-war era, is in every sense the antithesis of its restless neighbourhood. The front is a smooth concrete wall interrupted only by the entrance, it both attracts the gaze and repels it, creating a strong visual appeal.

The internal organisation of the house is based on a centripetal principle. A courtyard forms the spatial and imagined centre point of the tripartite floor plan. All of the rooms in the house are arranged around it in a way that guarantees the maximum amount of privacy. Light flooding the entrance area from above mediates between the interior and the street—a gesture made by a house whose "architecture of the wall" (Masao Furuyama) undeniably harbours a certain socio-critical potential (see also Ilka & Andreas Ruby's essay, p. 20). ›

Azuma House, Row House, Sumiyoshi, Japan 1975–76 The introverted block of the Azuma House adopts a clear stance in the heterogeneous row of houses along the street. Whereas the neighbouring buildings open outwards, Ando's house is oriented towards an internal courtyard at the centre of the tripartite floor plan, which offers connections on both levels between the different spaces in the house.

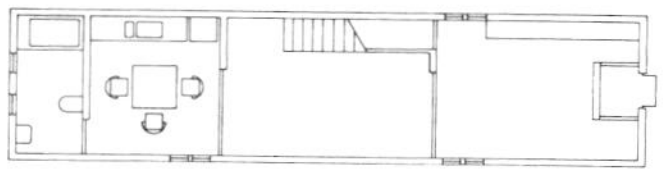

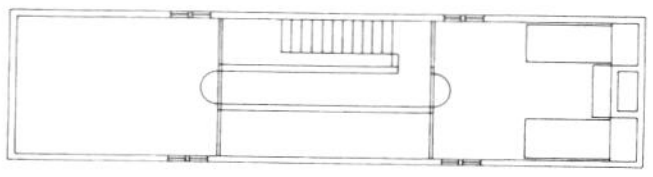

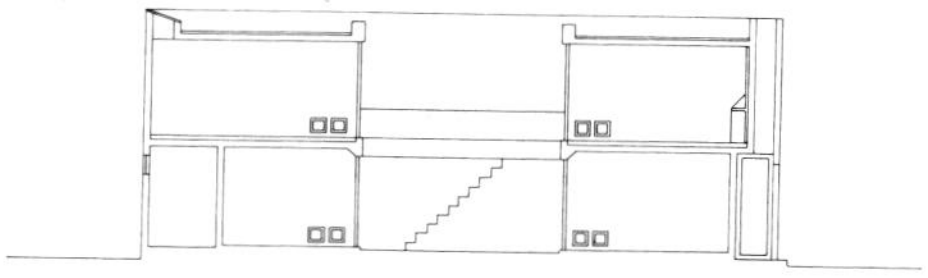

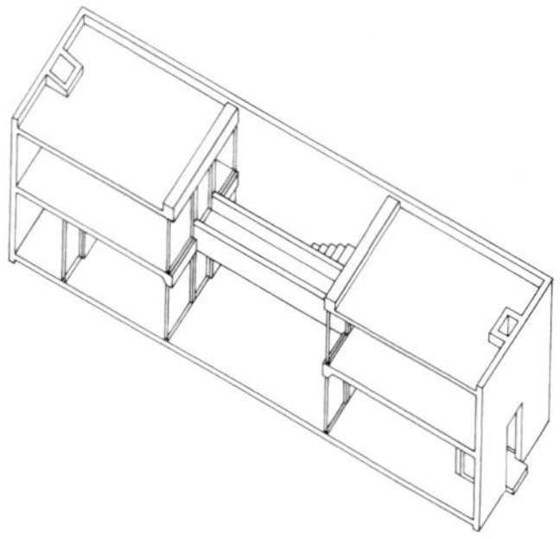

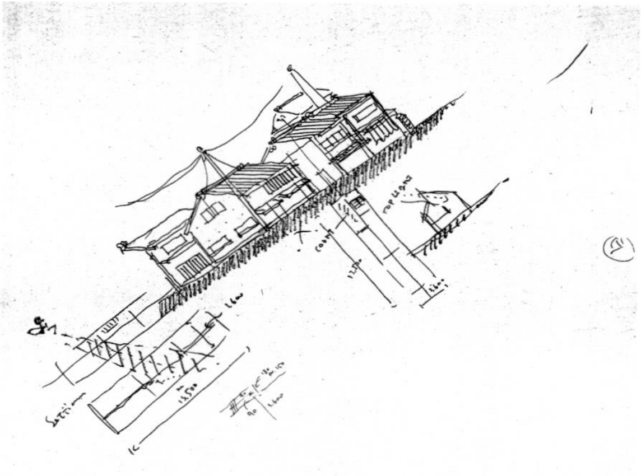

Although from the mid-1980s onwards Tadao Ando's buildings start to open outwards, his Church of the Light in Ibaraki, Osaka from 1987–89 represents a further example of a concrete box that is, for the most part, closed to the outside. The rectangular floor plan is sliced at an angle of 15 degrees by a freestanding wall separating the entrance area from the church space. Into the altar wall Ando cut a cross that extends to the sidewalls allowing light to enter the otherwise almost dark space.

Light in its sculptural form is the decisive element in this space that is inclined slightly towards the altar and whose floor and church pews are made of simple dark wooden boards. Using radical abstraction and reduction Ando has succeeded in creating one of the most transcendental church spaces in recent architecture. ›

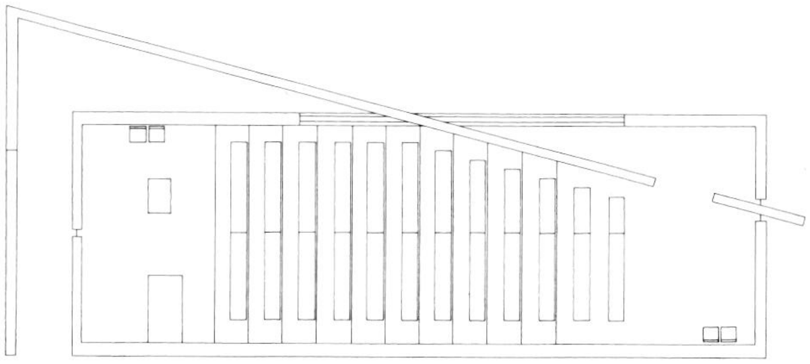

Church of the Light, Ibaraki, Osaka, Japan 1987–89 By its changing intensity, its reflections and the contrast it makes with the shadows, the light entering the church suggests to the visitor not only the Christian symbol of the Cross but also the cycles of time and of nature.

Not unusual for a museum building the Pulitzer Foundation for the Arts in St. Louis, Missouri is a project with a lengthy history extending from the start of planning in 1992 to completion in 2001. It is a recent example of Tadao Ando's uncompromisingly reduced architectural language. The museum is part of a scheme to revitalise central St. Louis and is intended to become the focus of the city's cultural zone. The project has a residential scale, the simple composition consists of two rectangular volumes of different heights, both made of fair-faced concrete, that enclose a water garden. The taller element contains the main exhibition hall while the lower one—housing entrance area, administration and research facilities—has a roof garden on top. The building has numerous carefully calculated openings that create a close relationship between inside and outside, provide light for the exhibition spaces and allow an awareness of the passage of time and the change of the seasons. □

Angeli Sachs

Pulitzer Foundation for the Arts, St. Louis, Missouri, USA 1992–2001 The museum, which was established as a private foundation, consists of two parallel volumes of fair-faced concrete and, by and large, closes itself off from urban space. Its hermetic exterior forms a contrast to the concept of the relationship between internal and external space that is particularly evident in the water garden and the roof terrace (see also ill. on p. 36).

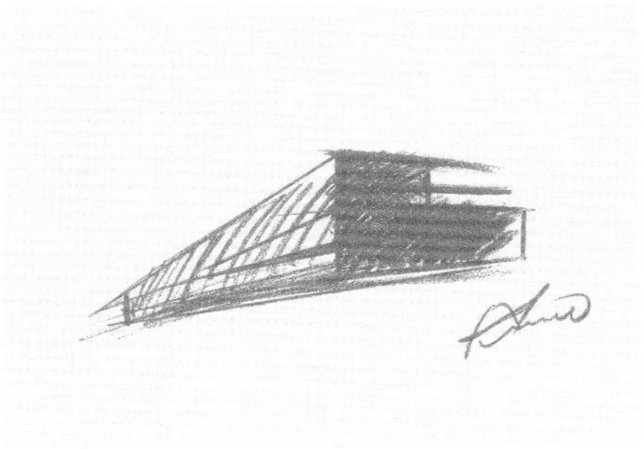

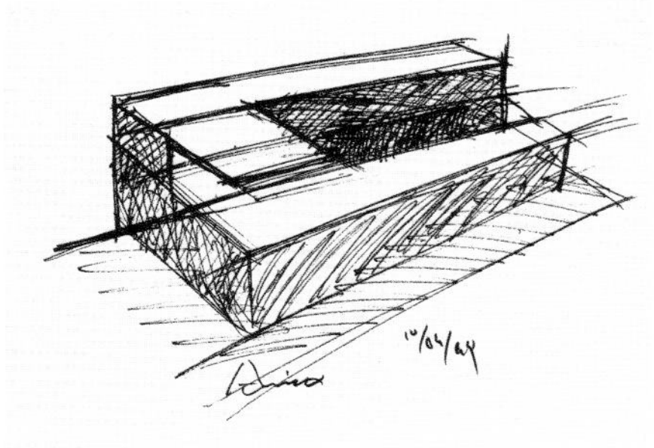

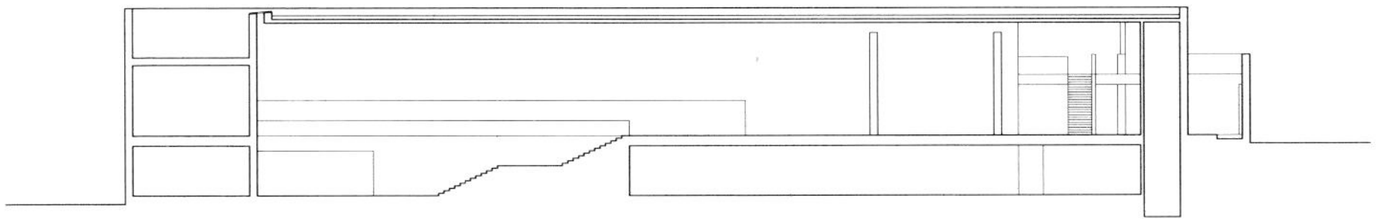

Tadao Ando

Pulitzer Foundation for the Arts, St. Louis, Missouri, USA 1992–2001 In Tadao Ando's architectural concept the Pulitzer Foundation is intended as a place of constant stimulation and of exchange between visitors, museum, artists and artworks. Richard Serra and Ellsworth Kelly, who are represented in the collection by important works, were involved in the design process of the institution that has a floor area of over 2,380 square metres and they contributed to achieving a balanced relationship between architecture and art.

Herzog & de Meuron I

With their Ricola Storage Building in Laufen, Switzerland (1987) which was immediately followed by the Stone House in Tavole, Italy (1982–88) Herzog & de Meuron laid, quite literally, the foundation stone of what was subsequently to be described in Switzerland as minimalist architecture. The building was understood as an alternative to both the logic of Deconstructivism and also to the kind of post-modern architecture based on quoting various styles. Every kind of typological and stylistic association appears to rebound from this building's facades. In contrast to most of their colleagues, even at that date Herzog & de Meuron were not interested in reduction in the sense of the classical modernist tradition. This project is located much closer to the premises of American Minimal Art. Like the interior of Donald Judd's steel cubes which remain unseen and, as physical space, are not the issue—a fact that led to the reproach from a number of critics that his works were "hollow" or "theatrical"—Herzog & de Meuron suppress the interior of the fully automated high rack warehouse that was fitted out by a specialist company. To them, the space seems to be "squeezed out" of the warehouse. Their interest is concentrated on "exhibiting" the facade by, literally, stacking the cladding of fibre-cement panels on wooden battens, not unlike a *Stack* by Donald Judd. The wall is thus an additive collection and layering of the materials of which it is made. The architects are, however, not concerned with the "authenticity" of the materials but rather with their semantic potential. Additionally the materials mediate between the function of storage inside the building and the process of geological sedimentation as it is visible along the face of a disused stone quarry near the building. ›

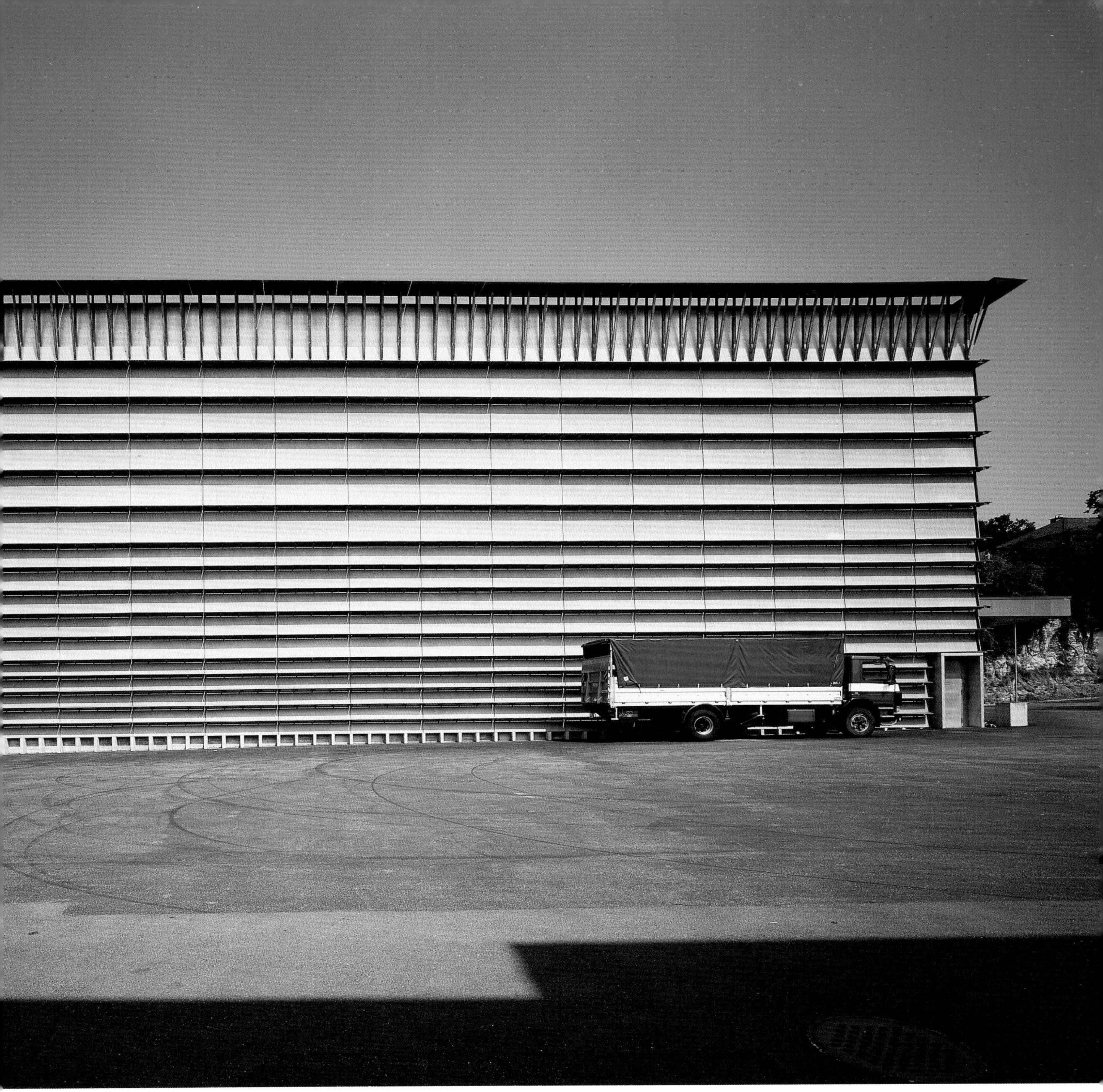

Ricola Storage Building, Laufen, Switzerland 1986–87 The project is the first of several projects by Herzog & de Meuron for the world's leading herbal candy producer. The Eternit panels are larger at the top than at the bottom where the facade appears to be supported by a series of foundations. The cantilevered timber construction in the upper part makes the galvanised sheet-metal box visible that delimitates the inside of the actual storage hall.

Goetz Collection, Gallery for a Private Collection of Modern Art, Munich, Germany 1989–92
The gallery, which is located in the garden of a private mansion, houses an important collection of international art of the 1970s, '80s and '90s. The artist, Helmut Federle, collaborated with the architects in conceiving the gallery spaces.

Shortly after the completion of the Ricola Storage Building Herzog & de Meuron started planning the building which, for many commentators, is the example par excellence of minimalist architecture: the Goetz Collection, Gallery for a Private Collection of Modern Art in Munich, Germany (1989–92) which indeed stands in its small garden like a monumental Minimal Art sculpture. The geometric basic form, the choice of materials: birch plywood panels, aluminium and opaque glass, as well as the serial arrangement of the panels recall the design principles and the "look" of Minimal Art. The construction —it essentially consists of two containers stacked one above the other—is simple but the phenomenological effects are highly diverse. It is difficult to work out the composition of the building from outside as its surfaces gives it a enigmatic quality. In contrast to the Ricola Storage Building the architects also designed the interior of this building yet it remains without any obvious connection to the outside. On account of the high position of the windows it is difficult to know on which storey you find yourself. Furthermore, the staircase forms an autonomous spatial system. Its structural arrangement, which resembles interlocking drawers, contrasts with the calm exhibition spaces. It allows the visitors to physically experience that the architects are not concerned with simplification but with creating something highly complex out of what appears to be ordinary. □

Philip Ursprung

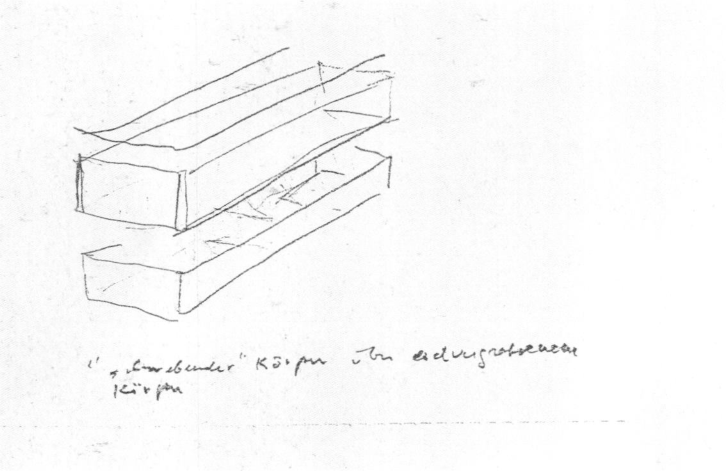

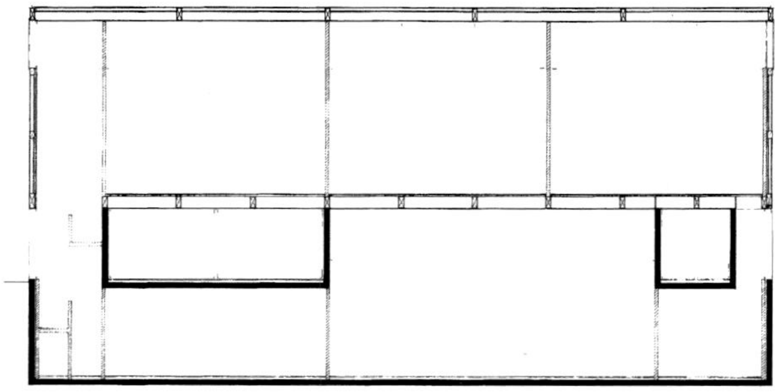

Goetz Collection, Gallery for a Private Collection of Modern Art, Munich, Germany 1989–92 A timber structure rests on a reinforced concrete base that is half buried. As the architects wrote on an early sketch made in 1989: "'Floating' structure over structure buried in the earth." The reinforced concret tubes are set laterally between the lower and upper galleries. The larger of the two serves as the office and reception area.

Annette Gigon and Mike Guyer achieved their international breakthrough with their museum extension building in Winterthur, Switzerland (1993–95). This project can be effortlessly positioned close to a number of principles of Minimal Art. As a temporary building it is—at least theoretically—a building for a limited time which, by means of its emphatically contemporary appearance, or its "look" as minimal artists would have said, is clearly distinguished from the older museum building dating from 1913.

The theme of expansion, so critically important for Minimal Art, is also evoked by this project. The extension was subject to considerable economic pressure. The ground floor area had to be preserved as a car park but instead of disguising this use, which seems at first glance so much at loggerheads with the project, the architects in fact profited from it. The museum simply incorporated the car park. Both museum and car park were clad with simple Profilit structural glazing panels.

Whereas the exterior of the museum building recalls Minimal Art's flirt with serialism and the sobriety of industrial materials the interior seems at a first glance to be a sequence of neutral white cubes. But the impression of an absolute space is deceptive. Three large windows interrupt the hermetic enclosure of the interior and open up a view to the outside. Framed by the window opening we see fine, mature trees typical of the Winterthur area. Once a centre of the Swiss machine industry, this town has preserved to the present day a number of late nineteenth-century villas built by factory owners. The mature trees in the gardens of these houses recall better days and also illustrate the fact that, following the disappearance of industry, Winterthur's identity is being newly defined by projects such as that by Gigon / Guyer. ›

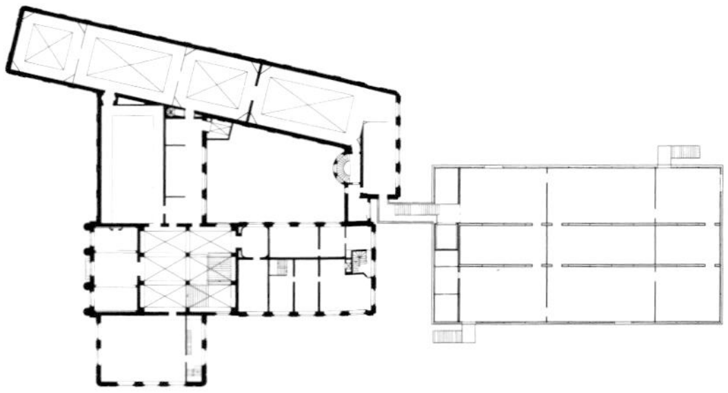

Extension of the Winterthur Museum of Art, Winterthur, Switzerland 1993–95
The annex to the Kunstmuseum Winterthur was realized as a temporary extension. The new building is connected to the older one by Rittmeyer & Furrer by a passageway. It offers an additional 1,000 square metres of exhibition space. Its high rooms are lit by sawtooth skylights.

Similar to the way in which the museum extension directs our attention to the surroundings and their history Gigon/Guyer's Stellwerk Vorbahnhof (Switching Station) at the Zurich perimeter train station (1996–99) also plays with the specific qualities of the site. What many might regard as an unexciting commission has, at the latest since Herzog & de Meuron's Signal Box, Auf dem Wolf in Basel (p. 70), been revealed as an opportunity for architecture to shape the appearance of the transport infrastructure in urban peripheral zones that is normally determined exclusively by functional requirements.

The dust caused by the trains braking has given all buildings near the tracks a rust-red patina. The architects coloured their concrete building using the same material—iron oxide pigments (colour concept by artist Harald F. Müller). The monolithic building seems to alternately dissolve and solidify in the flickering, constantly changing environment. What goes on inside the building remains a puzzle. The supervisors who work on the upper floor remain invisible, the metallic coated panes of the signal box windows reflect the surroundings. This building, perhaps only semi-consciously registered by many travellers out of the corner of the eye, is an up-to-date monument of that industrial sublime so important to Minimal Art, a mixture of the threat and the beauty of industrial phenomena. □

Philip Ursprung

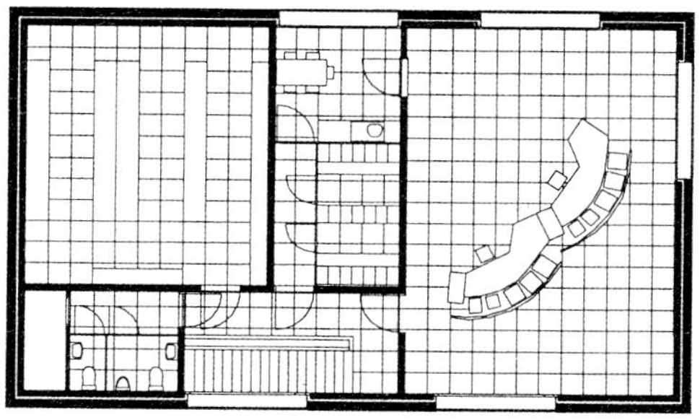

Switching Station, Zurich, Switzerland 1996–99 On the inside of the three-story building, only the upper floor is used as a working area and recreational room for the employees. The lower floors house the technical installations. The envelope is a double-hulled concrete construction. It allows for temperature control of the interior. Furthermore, the concrete reinforcing bars function as a Faraday cage in order to protect the sensitive electronics inside the building from exterior disturbances.

Adolf Krischanitz

The Neue Welt School (1992–94), a Jewish kindergarten in the Prater—designed by Austrian architect Adolf Krischanitz in conjunction with painter Helmut Federle, who was responsible for the choice of materials and colours—has become Vienna's best known "black box". This concrete building, part of which hovers on a plateau, is distinguished by its clarity of structure and homogeneity. It is an addition of rectangular elements of different sizes, arranged and designed in such a way that, as Otto Kapfinger put it, "a restrained energy of inner motion" develops.

In contrast to many other buildings of Essential Minimalism the Neue Welt School is not an externally closed box whose internal life remains concealed. The minimalist interiors are in fair-faced concrete, the rear walls of the group rooms and the sidewalls of the corridor are yellowish green surfaces, in contact with the outer world they tend towards green. This contact is made possible by large window openings, extending down to the floor, that place the building in a close and varied relationship with the outdoors and create a play between inside and outside. The apparently black facade is, in fact, saturated in the colour of lava stone and, like the entire building, reacts to changes in the light and the surrounding vegetation. The Neue Welt School is a rare example of a piece of architecture that applies Minimal Art's principle of dissolving the boundaries around the object and allowing it to expand into the space surrounding it. ›

Neue Welt School, Vienna, Austria 1992–94 Alongside the external form and the dramatic dark colouring of the facades the correspondence between inside and outside is one of the most prominent characteristics of the Neue Welt School. Placed on a site with mature trees, the building's exchange with the colours of the vegetation and the sky is assisted by Helmut Federle's colour concept for the interior.

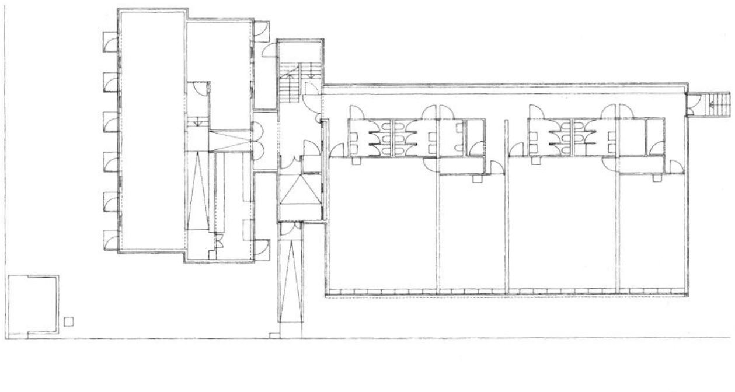

Neue Welt School, Vienna, Austria 1992–94
The trees surrounding the clearly articulated building of the Neue Welt School are reflected in its large window openings. This leads to a complex perception, a multivalent image in which, on the one hand, the walls are emphasised as defining elements and, on the other, the building also appears permeable.

Temporary buildings and exhibition pavilions represent a special aspect of Adolf Krischanitz' work. The Kunsthalle project space on Karlsplatz in Vienna (2000–02) is the successor of an earlier building for the Kunsthalle on the same site erected by Krischanitz between 1990–92 and later removed. The Kunsthalle has moved to Vienna's new Museumsquartier but has allowed itself the luxury of the project space at its old location as a satellite for young, yet-to-be established art. Located at the centre of Vienna's heterogeneous Karlsplatz, which is dissected by busy traffic arteries, the considerably smaller new building is conceived as a transparent hovering box, which reveals its contents not only to the visitors who manage to reach this island haven but also presents them, like a film cut, to motorists driving by. The flexible interior can be subdivided as required. A wall running the length of the building separates the exhibition area from the highly popular café, the cash desk, the bookshop and the office. The simplicity of the materials and the temporary character of the exhibition building create an exciting contrast to the classic elegance of the glass box. □

Angeli Sachs

Kunsthalle II—project space, Vienna, Austria 2000–02 Positioned like an island at the centre of this urban space, with an appearance that fluctuates between improvisation and permanence, the pavilion forming the new project space of the Kunsthalle Wien places a clear accent in the heterogeneous ambiance of Karlsplatz that is criss-crossed by major traffic arteries.

Standardised Buildings for Railway Technology,
various locations throughout Switzerland 1995–2001

Since the mid-1990s passengers travelling on Swiss trains may have noticed small monolithic, almost black, buildings lining the routes. Like the areas beside the tracks, on the edge of which they are located, they seem to have been left to their own devices. Grass has grown up around several of them and they have acquired that rusty, sooty patina characteristic of the railway landscape. Around fifty of these so-called Normierte Gebäude für Bahntechnik, SBB (Standardised Buildings for Railway Technology, Swiss Federal Railways) were built by Morger & Degelo between 1995 and 2001. They are neither definitely architecture nor sculpture, they are not pure infrastructure nor buildings with a representative function, neither one-offs nor ubiquitous mass products. In fact these projects maintain a precarious balance between different categories. In a certain way they continue the discussion about the boundaries between painting and sculpture which Donald Judd started in the 1960s when he coined the mysterious term "specific object".

In 2000 Meinrad Morger, Heinrich Degelo and Christian Kerez built the Kunstmuseum Liechtenstein (Liechtenstein Art Museum) in Vaduz, a building that embodies in an exemplary approach the values of Swiss Minimalism. As was typical of minimalist projects by Diener & Diener, Meili & Peter, and Peter Zumthor towards the end of the 1980s, in the Liechtenstein art museum the outer shell and the interior are also conceived completely independently of each other. The project is a monumental black box (Hans Frei), in which everything is concentrated on the celebration of a spectacular surface. The facade seems to have been cast in a single pour. By sanding down the raw concrete a surface with a polished sheen was created in which the surroundings are reflected. It seems as if the architects, by sanding the concrete also wanted to eradicate every kind of typological association, every reference to the context until nothing was left but a timeless, autonomous form that refers only to itself. It is precisely the example of the Liechtenstein Art Museum that enables us to illustrate how greatly the premises of minimalist architects differ from those of the protagonists of Minimal Art in the 1960s. In contrast to Minimal Art where simple interventions led to complex visual effects, in the case of Morger Degelo and Kerez a complicated, expensive intervention is used to create a simple visual effect, i.e. reflection. ›

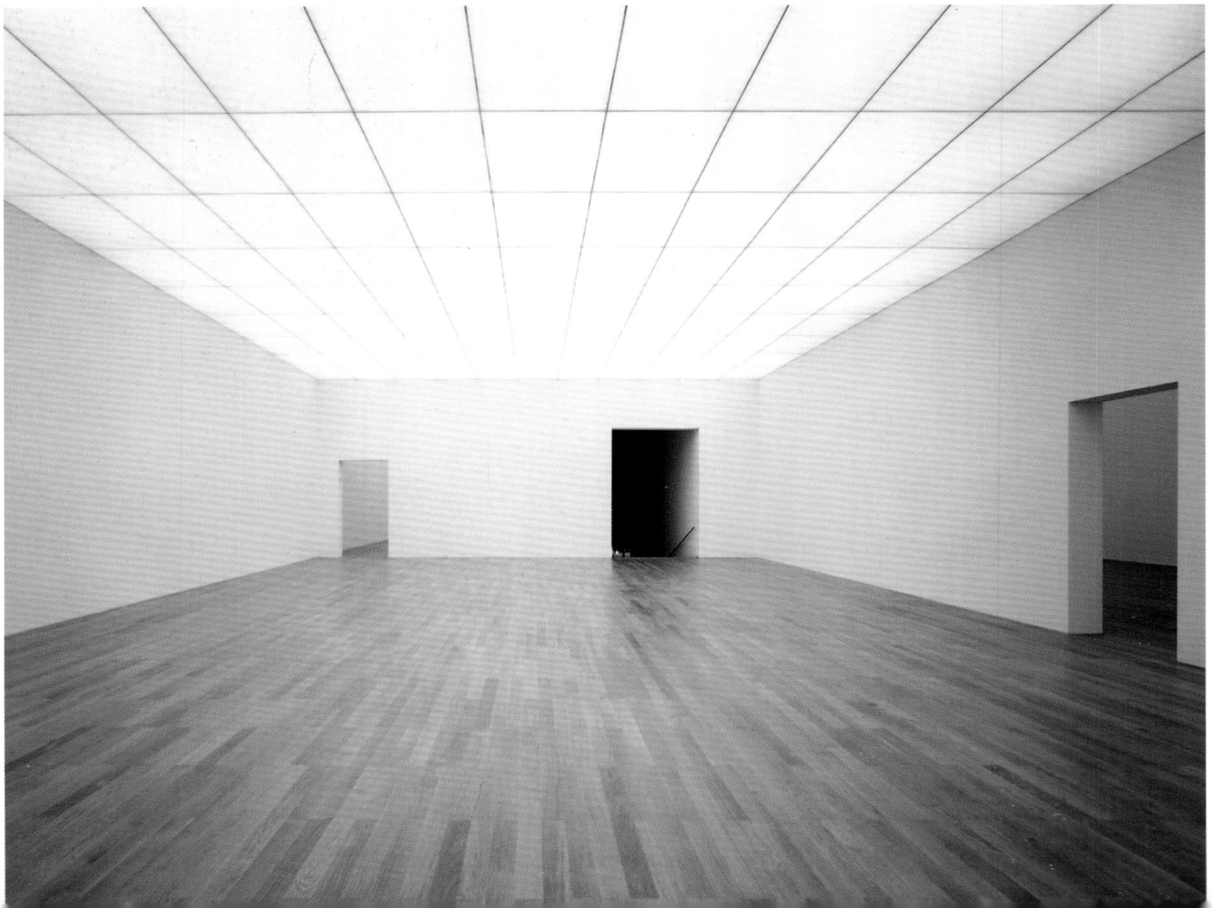

Liechtenstein Art Museum, Vaduz, Liechtenstein 1998–2000 Typical for the museum boom in the 1990s, the museum was financed by a joint venture of private sponsors and the State of Liechtenstein. It houses the renowned collections of the Count of Liechtenstein and the Liechtensteinische Staatliche Kunstsammlungen. It also functions as an exhibition space for temporary exhibitions.

Handicraft that is the very practice which minimal artists wished to delegate and make invisible is here ascribed a central significance. Like a rough diamond which first becomes fully visible and valuable through precise cutting and polishing the surface of this museum had to undergo a lengthy process of transformation. Consequently this project is subject to an aesthetic economy of values based on refining and sublimating, on compressing and abstracting which may well apply to high modernist art such as Brancusi's sculptures but which is something the minimal artists of the 1960s wished to overcome. □

Philip Ursprung

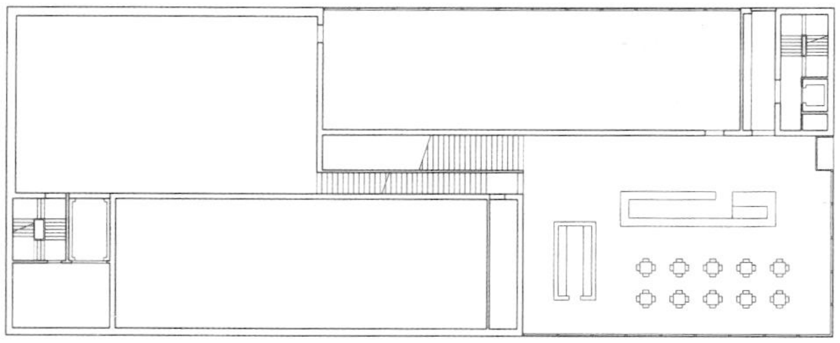

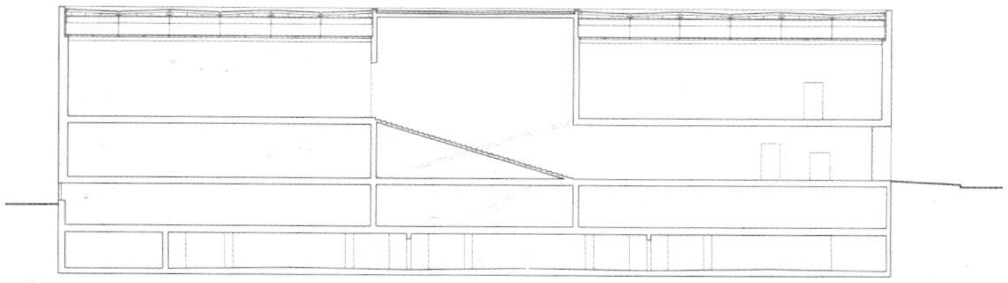

Liechtenstein Art Museum, Vaduz, Liechtenstein 1998–2000
The building's highly-polished surface consists of course aggegrate concrete using river pebbles from the Rhine.

Diener & Diener

If we take a look at the work of those Swiss architects that can, in one way or another be associated with minimal architecture, in the case of Diener & Diener's projects the striking thing is the emphasis on the urban reference and the careful processing of the context in which their buildings, despite their minimalist forms, so confidently insert themselves. Martin Steinmann, who probably has made the most intensive analysis of their architectural approach, writes in *The House and the City* as follows about the way their buildings present themselves: "In the older plans of Diener & Diener it is the forms or signs that define a place ... In the new ones such parameters are not simply disregarded—the site remains decisive—but it is more general qualities that are now brought to expression, properties such as 'density' or 'gravity' or their opposite, and they are expressed in an idiom which is reduced to a minimum."

The same can be said of their exciting urban intervention at the seam between Lucerne's old town and the front onto Lake Lucerne. The new building for a supermarket of the major Swiss retailer Migros (1995–2000) combines the monumental forms of the basilica, derived from the market hall type, which here also establishes a reference to the neighbouring church, with a radically reduced formal language that is expressed both in the stringent overall structure and the modular organisation of the facade made of oxidised copper panels and glass in which striking window openings are cut. This shimmering green block asserts itself as an independent built sculpture in a heterogeneous environment that it even rearranges in a subtle way. ›

Migros Shopping Centre and Klubschule (Adult Education Institute), Lucerne, Switzerland 1995–2000
The new building for the Migros supermarket is part of a restructuring programme that affects the ensemble of the Schweizerhof hotel and its surroundings in the old town. The project included the renovation of the hotel and the adjoining function rooms, a new Migros supermarket building and a Migros Klubschule. Inside the reinforced concrete frame structure, which allows a completely flexible organisation of the sales area, the colourful world of the goods on sale forms a contrast to the building's minimalist formal language.

KIND
HÖRZENTRALE
• Hörgeräte
• Hörtest
• Batterien
BROT

Amsterdam's eastern port area that had outlived its original function is the subject of one of the largest and most ambitious urban development projects of recent times in the Netherlands. The city decided not to build any further office districts but to transform the four peninsulas KNSM, Java, Borneo and Sporenburg into residential areas. Jo Coenen's master plan emphasises the urban character of the new quarter by increasing density and by the use of block structures and block perimeter development.

In 1995 Diener & Diener won a competition for one of the most important areas of the new housing district, the transitional area between the peninsulas KNSM and Java that is also the point at which this double peninsula is accessed from the inner city. Diener & Diener defined this situation using two different kinds of buildings: a recessed courtyard type and a long building that is articulated into three parts by setbacks in the long facades, erected directly on filled ground at the water's edge. The relationship to the surroundings is established by the clearly expressed structure and the brick cladding to the facades. Above all the long building, that uses only one kind of opening, attracts attention by its balance between monumentality and minimalist reserve. On alternate floors the window openings are shifted laterally half a brick to the left or the right so that they are out of line vertically with the row of openings above and below; although almost imperceptible this creates a certain movement in the facade. ›

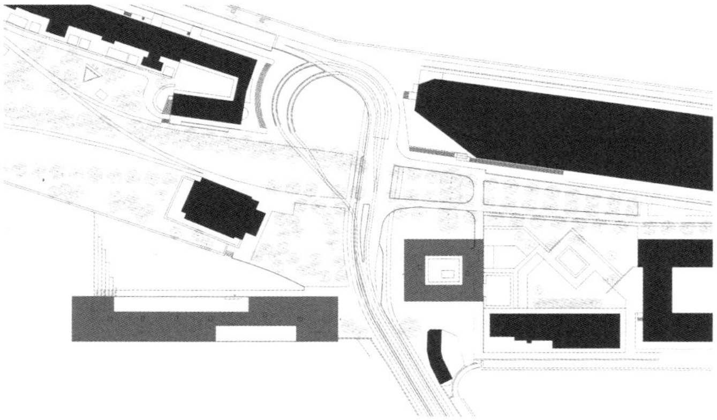

KNSM- and Java-Island Apartment Blocks, Amsterdam, The Netherlands 1995–2001 In the site plan and the overall view we see the long building (on the left) and the courtyard building (at the centre) in the context of the surrounding, partly historical, development. On the right the window openings of the long building appear completely uniform but in fact each horizontal row of openings is slightly staggered so that the verticals do not line up.

RuhrMuseum Zollverein Colliery (project), Essen, Germany 1999–2002

The Zollverein colliery near Essen was built between 1929 and 1932 in the *Neues Bauen* style (1920s German modernism) by architects Fritz Schupp and Martin Kremmer. In 2001 it was inscribed in the UNESCO world cultural heritage list and is the most important monument in the Ruhr area from the era of large-scale mining. Over a period of time the buildings of this ensemble—that was closed down in 1986—have, one after the other, been given new functions in the areas of culture and communications. The largest building in the colliery will accommodate the RuhrMuseum, a regional natural history and culture museum. In 1999 Diener & Diener emerged as victors from a competition for this project with their concept of adding a floor to the building while leaving the substance of the monument in the interior untouched. In a reworking of the project in 2002 in addition to the museum a visitor centre for the complex was integrated in the old coal washing building. The added floor of glass transforms the historic building into a sculpture that is both minimalist and monumental and which proclaims from afar that the old substance deemed worthy of preservation has been given a new function and presence. Unfortunately, this project will not be realised. □

Angeli Sachs

RuhrMuseum Zollverein Colliery (project), Essen, Germany 1999–2002
In this design the visitor centre of the Zollverein colliery is to be located at ground floor level of the coal washing building. Originally washed coal and waste deposits were loaded onto wagons waiting here. Below is a section through the building in its new function.

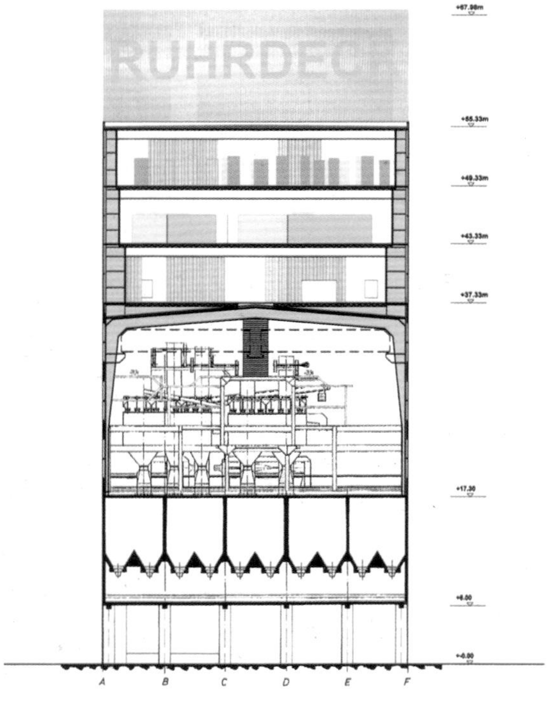

design 200

12 000 T
KOHLE
PRO TAG
Geologie
Mineralogie
Paläontologie
und ich
mittendrin
2-museumsnacht
27.06.02
WERDEN
200 T STAHL
ZUR
AUSSTEIFUNG
EINGEBAUT

Projects II Whereas Minimal Art is a genuinely American art phenomenon, the discussion on minimalist architecture in the 1990s took place entirely in Europe and Japan. What was the reason for this? Was it the wish of some young architects to hide behind the protective shield offered by "art" or "America" in order to avoid the difficulties caused by the modernist inheritance and to develop in peace an alternative to Deconstructivism and Postmodernism? Did they perhaps wish to establish a temporary home there like the hermit crab that occupies an empty mollusc shell in order to camouflage itself during its vulnerable growth phase?

Whatever the various motives may have been: the shell is no longer needed as within a short space of time a series of corresponding architectural positions has been established in Europe and the USA that handle Minimal Art as a reference in an increasingly unencumbered and unbiased manner. The way the building surface is currently treated is almost like an indication of the exfoliation process architecture has recently undergone. Membrane-like, often shimmering surfaces that appear to be stretched like a skin around the building are dominant. Some seem vulnerable; others are iridescent producing complex visual effects.

The more often the term minimalism was used by architecture critics in the course of the 1990s, the more vague its meaning became. Architects such as Herzog & de Meuron were soon to protest against being associated with this term at all. The following projects have in common the fact that they re-evaluate the premises of minimalist architecture. In the case of many projects it is difficult from our perspective to trace the influence of Minimal Art. It is the quasi-artistic conceptual strategies with which architects reflect upon and expand existing positions that attract our attention rather than any formal similarities to actual works of art.

Philip Ursprung

Herzog & de Meuron II

The discussion of scale was one of the central questions of Minimal Art. But the impetus of this discussion soon reached its limits: whereas in exhibitions such as *Scale as Content* (1967) the museum architecture became a point of reference for the sculpture, with the exception of Mathias Goeritz's proto-minimalist interventions the protagonists of Minimal Art never succeeded in achieving urban dimensions in their work. The Signal Box, Auf dem Wolf in Basel (1989–94) by Herzog & de Meuron plays an important role in this context. As the control of rail traffic today is conducted exclusively by means of monitors it was possible to dispense almost completely with windows. The building is monolithic, almost "blind" and resembles the Black Box type so popular with the creators of Minimal Art in which the interior remains mysterious. Like a solenoid the entire building is wrapped by a band of copper ten centimetres wide. On the one hand the metal screens the electronic systems inside much like a Faraday cage, on the other this simple, easy to follow procedure creates an endless source of visual effects, light reflections and nuances of colour that change according to the time of day. Finally, but not least importantly the signal box functions as a monumental landmark linking the broad expanse of the tracks to the urban landscape. ›

Signal Box, Auf dem Wolf, Basel, Switzerland 1989–94 The building mainly houses electronic equipment on its six floors. Its concrete shell is insulated on the exterior. Ten-centimetre-wide copper strips are wrapped around it. At the point where they pass in front of the windows, they are slightly twisted in order to admit daylight. A central signal tower within sight of the signal box was completed in 1999. They form a pair and may later be expanded into a group.

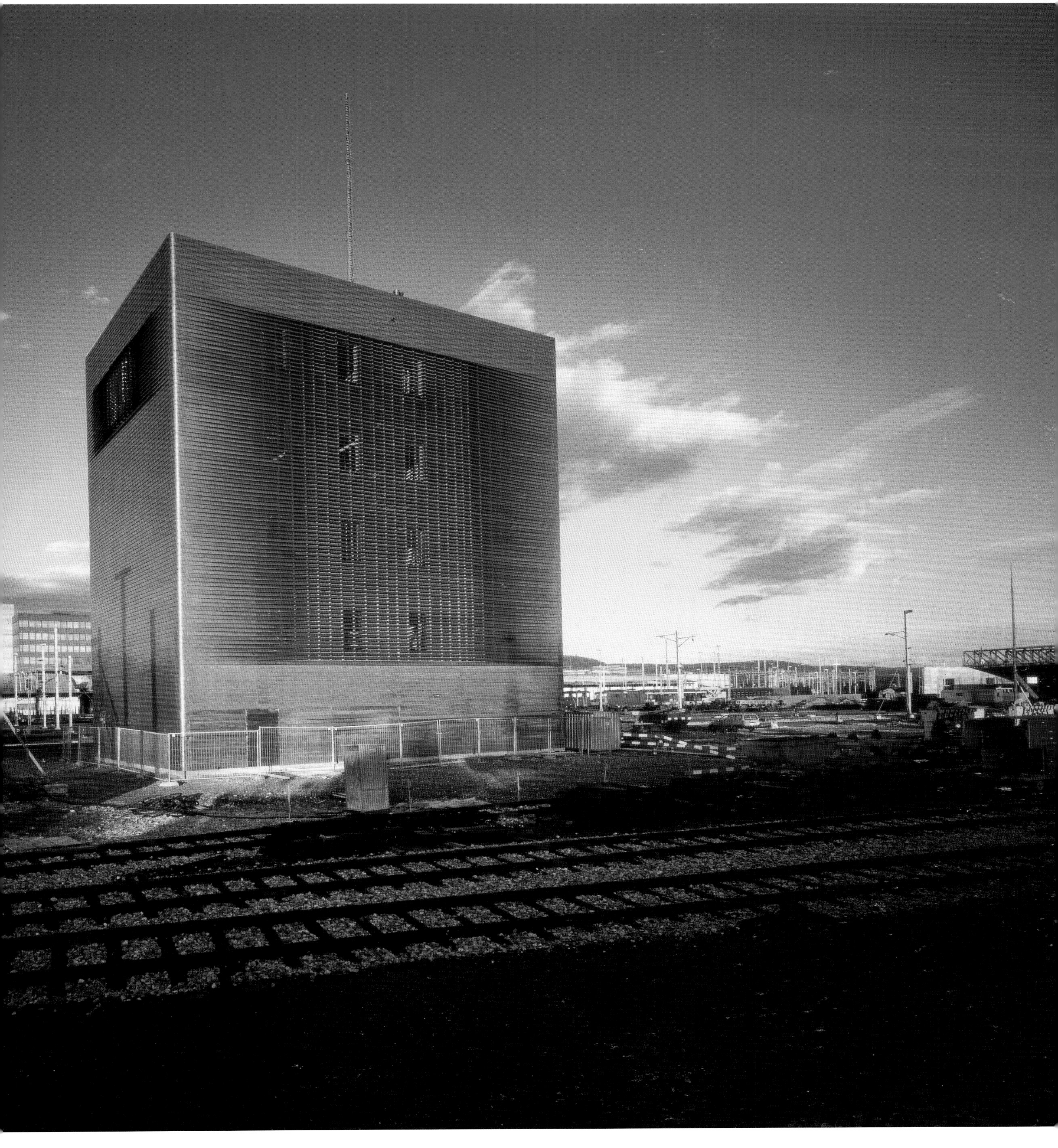

COSTAIN

Tate Modern, London, England 1995–2000

One of the qualities of Minimal Art as "post industrial" art was that it evoked memories of the world of heavy industry that in the 1960s was slowly disappearing. Hence its affinity to technoid structures, to metal, rust, prefabricated materials and industrial production processes. Hence the fact that the works of Minimal Art are particularly effective when displayed in factory halls emptied of their machinery. Hence also the way they function as contemporary backdrops which many critics in the 1960s rejected as "trendy" and "theatrical". One reason for the great success of Herzog & de Meuron's Tate Modern in London (1995–2000) is that the architects essentially did nothing other than empty the modernist power station. They left the brick facade largely intact, only the striking light beam placed on top of the building marks its transformation and underlines the horizontal extent of the complex. Herzog & de Meuron concentrated primarily on the interior, increasing the height of the empty hall by lowering the floor and leading the visitors into the building over a spectacular ramp. Similar to the way some minimalist sculptures articulate the spatial quality of a vanished industrial production or indeed even stage it, with just a few interventions Herzog & de Meuron evoke memories of the old power station. Visitors can look through narrow bay windows into the depths of the empty hall and thereby experience the fascination of the "industrial sublime" that in the 1960s was so important for artists such as Tony Smith. However, in the Tate Modern the issue is not to preserve the earlier substance or to make a fetish of it by the use of certain details and materials. The primary concern is to transform it into a theatre of life that relates to the here and now and is part of the flow of time. □

Philip Ursprung

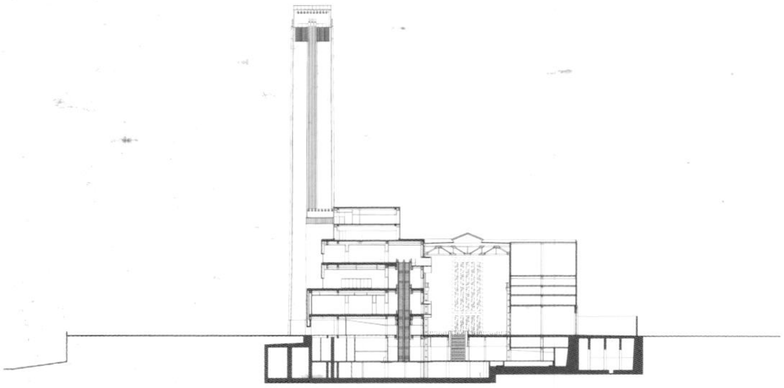

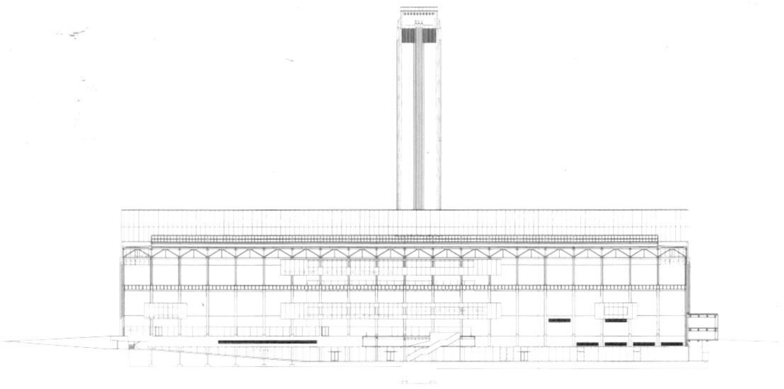

Tate Modern, London, England 1995–2000 The gigantic power station—designed by Giles Gilbert Scott—was decommissioned in 1982. The emptied turbine hall and the huge ramp, which descends gently from the west side were transformed into the central meeting point—a "landscape" as the architect put it. Visitors can relax and enjoy breathtaking views into the turbine hall from the bay windows. Seen from the ground floor, these windows appear like floating bodies of light and like showcases holding visitors in the galleries.

José Rafael Moneo

Despite the fact that his buildings have simple forms and surfaces treated in a purist manner to describe José Rafael Moneo as a minimalist architect would mean taking an unacceptably narrow view of his projects. What interests Moneo more than anything else is "building for the city" and to this end he develops an architectural language that adapts to suit its particular context. One of the best-known examples of this approach is his Museo Nacional de Arte Romano in Mérida (1980–85), that refers to the Roman remains of the town, which it abstracts and transforms into architecture. Despite these reservations about pigeon-holing his work it is true that the most exciting of his more recent projects, the Kursaal Auditorium and Congress Centre in San Sebastián dating from 1990–99, appears in almost all publications about minimalist architecture. This has to do with Moneo's response to the particular topographical situation of the Basque city of San Sebastián. The Kursaal lies at Concha Beach along a beautiful stretch of coastline and in a highly prominent position between the sea and the river. One of the initial requirements was that the new building should not impair the site's relationship to either the landscape or the city. Moneo's image for the two slightly inclined prismatic volumes that he sets on a platform above the beach is of "two gigantic rocks stranded at the mouth of the river forming part of the landscape rather than belonging to the city". ›

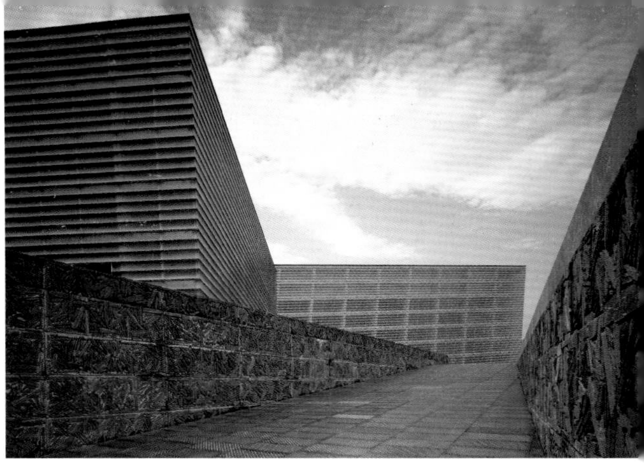

Kursaal Auditorium and Congress Centre, San Sebastián, Spain 1990–99
The expressive prismatic elements of the Kursaal add a special accent to the urban situation of San Sebastián that is characterised by a delightful harmony between city, sea and mountains. The larger of the two buildings contains the auditorium with seating for 1,806 visitors, the smaller one houses the Congress Centre. Their abstract form creates a link between the city and nature.

The larger of the two buildings contains the auditorium. It is designed as an almost completely closed cube, inside its slight asymmetry leads visitors almost automatically to the single window from which they have a view of the landscape. Otherwise the facade made of two glass layers provides a neutral bright interior in which the volume of the concert hall is inserted as a hovering element, so to speak. Externally the building appears as an almost opaque form that adapts itself to the changing light conditions and at night is a mysteriously shining cube of light. The same applies to the smaller, neighbouring congress hall.

If we wished to describe the two prismatic volumes of the Kursaal as minimalist architecture such a description could be justified by the compactness and clarity of the almost closed cubes and the way they are placed in their surroundings. Additionally, Moneo's imagery of the stranded rocks establishes an interesting link to Land Art. Yet at the same time the relationship of the two buildings to each other and to their setting, their dynamic quality and their expressiveness goes so far beyond the idea of "least is most" that the minimalist vocabulary here becomes part of a more complex context. ›

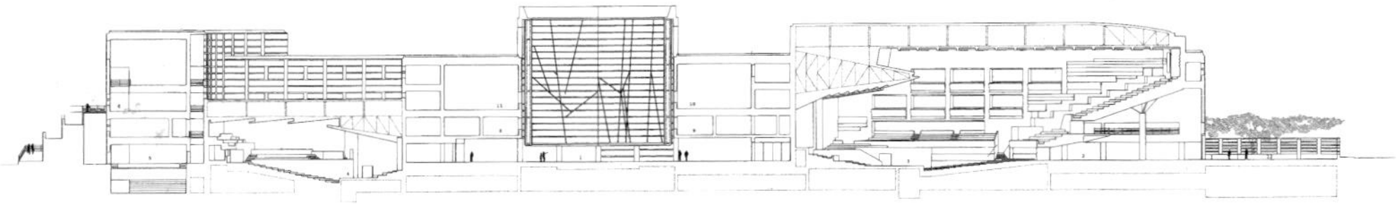

Kursaal Auditorium and Congress Centre, San Sebastián, Spain 1990–99 The design of the foyer creates a transition between the outside and the wooden clad spaces of the interior. The window in the foyer is part of the concept of linking art and nature and allows a panoramic view of the landscape.

Around the same time, Moneo built the Auditorium and Music Centre of Barcelona with its two concert halls (1988–99), which uses an entirely different formal language to the Kursaal. Here the minimalist principle of modular ordering is apparent. On the perimeter of the city's nineteenth-century expansion area and in a relatively diffuse urban situation, this long building asserts its autonomy by means of a complex reduced architecture and an interior that follows a clear plan with a precise handling of lines. The modular structure of the facade is created by a reinforced concrete frame infilled externally with panels of dark, reddish steel and, in contrast, with maple panels on the inside. The foyer is designed as a roofed public square dominated by a "lantern-impluvium". The structure of the facade is re-echoed by the boundary wall to the Auditorium and Music Centre site, a concrete frame that, in conjunction with the building, develops the qualities of a minimalist sculpture. □

Angeli Sachs

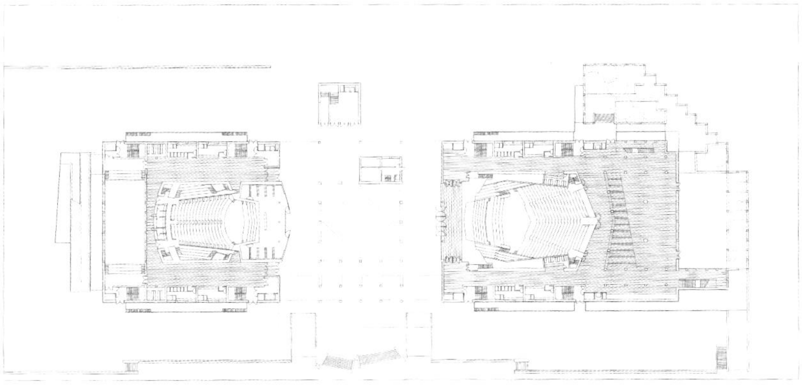

Auditorium and Music Centre, Barcelona, Spain 1988–99 This complex contains two concert halls, with seating for 2,340 and 610 people respectively, rehearsal rooms, a music museum, an educational institute, a specialist library and other facilities required to run this music centre. The foyer is designed as a public square that opens the building, which is conceived as a clear grid structure, to the public.

Academy for the Arts and Architecture, Maastricht, The Netherlands 1989–93 In a photo taken at night the modular structure of the Academy building is clearly revealed. The schematic visibility of what is happening inside mediates between the internal and external worlds.

With his Academy for the Arts and Architecture in Maastricht (1989–93) Wiel Arets implanted an initially alien element in the existing system of the city that is comparable to a virus which enters the human body and then causes changes within it (the analogy is from Arets himself). The extension to the Academy inserts itself into an existing ensemble at the same time creating a new urban space. This building, made up of modular units, drew a comparison from Kenneth Frampton with works of Minimal Art such as those by Donald Judd or Sol LeWitt and, as in their case, here a simple basic principle creates a rich diversity of effects. The facades consist primarily of glass blocks with different degrees of transparency that are fitted into a concrete frame made up of square bays, in addition at places a horizontal window is incised. Particularly when artificially-lit the interior of the Academy corresponds with the city outside, making the processes of movement, communication and work visible. Wiel Arets described this quality of his architecture in the following terms: "Architecture is therefore a between, a membrane, an alabaster skin, at once opaque and transparent, meaningful and meaningless, real and unreal." ("An Alabaster Skin") In the interior the academy is also marked by openness and at the same time by the industrial undertones supplied by the materials concrete and glass. The circulation system is entirely focussed on communication; from a single entrance a *promenade architecturale* leads through the different parts of the building that are connected with each other by a bridge. ›

Academy for the Arts and Architecture, Maastricht, The Netherlands 1989–93
The bridge connecting the parts of the building also follows the formal principles applied in the building as a whole. The minimalist fitting-out of the interior emphasises the building's workshop character and allows the users room for their own creativity.

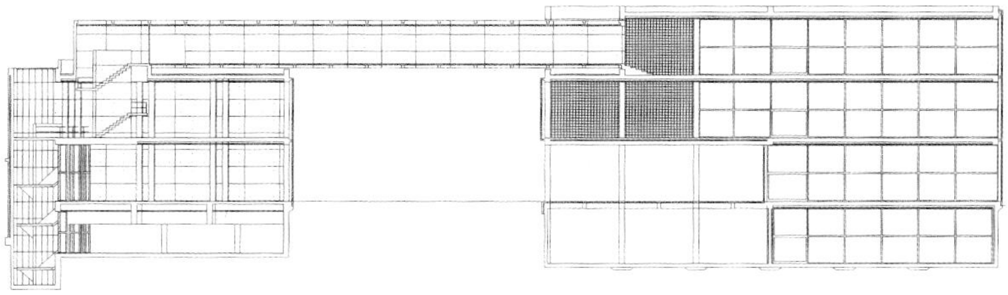

The Boxtel Police Station (1994–97) is also characterised by the principle of openness which in this particular case the Netherlands police wished to appropriate as their new corporate identity. This opening up to the outside and making administrative processes visible, however, had to be reconciled with the necessary security requirements. The police station consists of several elements that are combined to produce a "gleaming, icy, alien body" (Wiel Arets). The facade is made of standardised panels of matt, translucent glass connected to the structure by an aluminium frame; additional small, incised windows introduce a further element to the dialectic between permeability and closure. To allow an awareness from outside of the processes occurring in the interior of the building Arets refers to new information technology and animated images. ›

Police Station, Boxtel, The Netherlands 1994–97 This police station, a composition of various volumes, plays with the different effects created by the facade that has an industrial feel suggested by opaque and translucent elements.

This particular effect is intensified in the Lensvelt Offices and Factory Building in Breda (1995–99). The long, flat building for a furniture factory corresponds with the surrounding landscape which is also flat. As in Boxtel the facade consists of strips of translucent glass that allow those driving past on the surrounding roads schematic views of the processes in its interior that are like brief cuts from a film. Two box-like structures forming the entrance area place counterpoints to the extended main block of the factory.

Common to all three buildings is that the boundary between inside and outside is, at places, dissolved. All three consequently become constantly changing sculptures whose internal life is projected outside, allowing a complex aesthetic experience. □

Angeli Sachs

Lensvelt Offices and Factory Building, Breda, The Netherlands 1995–99 Motorists driving past the Lensvelt factory experience the elongated building and its translucent facade like a strip of film.

Claus en Kaan

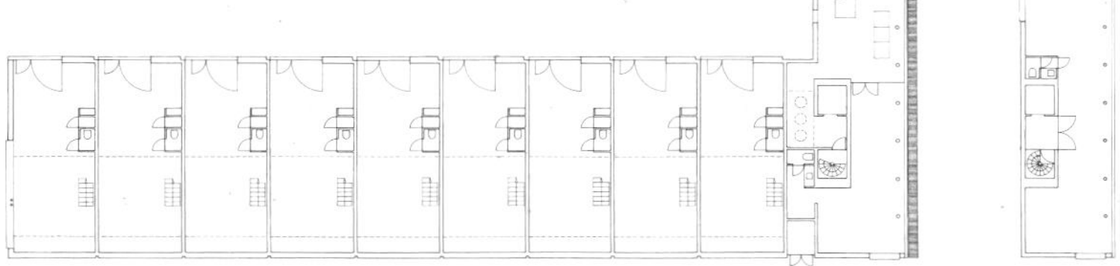

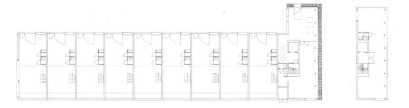

Eurotwin Business Centre, Amsterdam, The Netherlands 1992–93 This business complex consists of office units measuring 860 square metres and industrial units with a floor area of 1,880 square metres. The brief envisaged inexpensive accommodation for new companies. The facades made of strips of wood and horizontal glazing emphasise the building's abstract character.

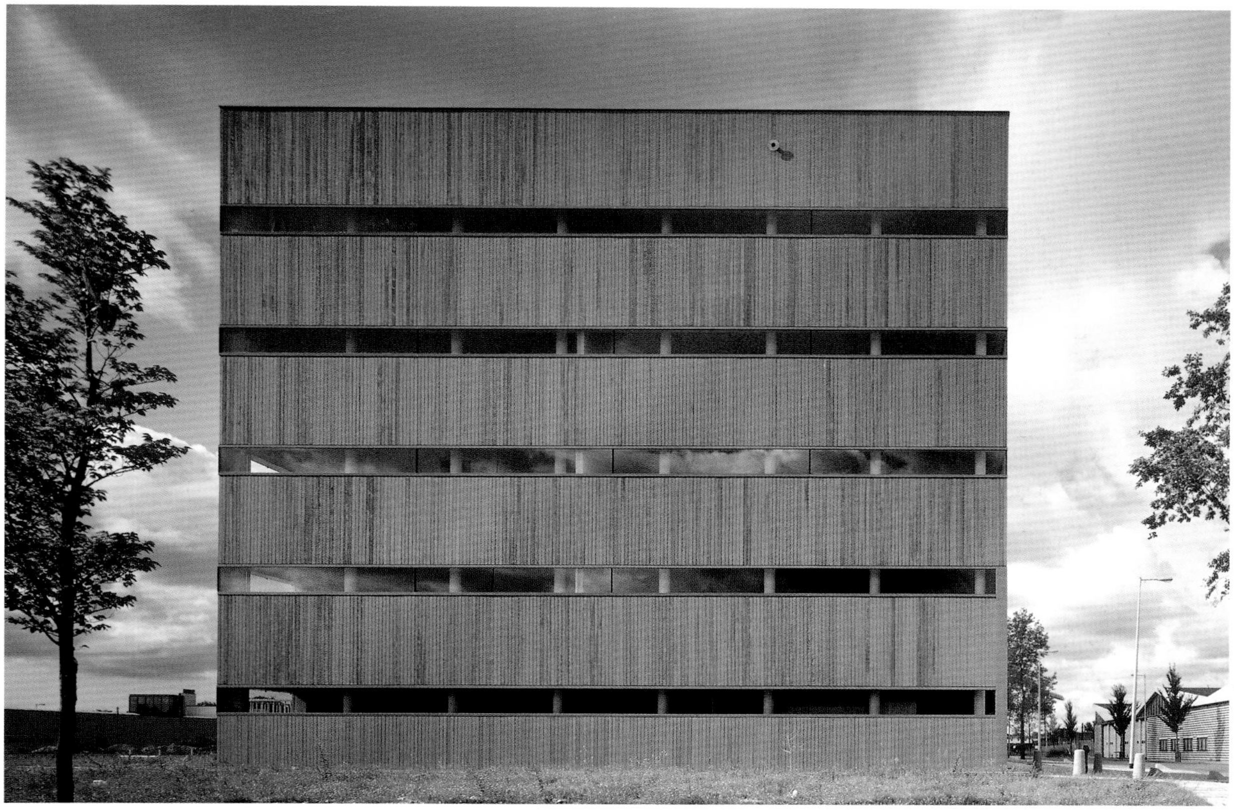

Claus en Kaan's architecture, characterised as it is by simplicity, seems easy to understand. It is not the outcome of a striving for originality or unusual forms but derives from a process of using an idea to achieve agreement between all involved. According to Felix Claus' and Kees Kaan's own statement: "The lack of autonomy in the design can result in considerable latitude for the designer". Rafael Moneo (see pp. 76–80), writes as follows about his Dutch colleagues: "There is in all the built work of Claus en Kaan a rejection of rhetoric that would lead us to conclude that they possess the puritan, contented distance of those who understand that it is not essential to enlist the help of the superfluous. Nothing in their work is unnecessary; it contains only what is right and necessary."

In addition to the continuity of idea rather than form a further aspect of Claus en Kaan's architectural language is the way they incorporate elements of surprise and excitement resulting from the use and contrast of very different natural and industrial materials that are integrated in clear and, at places, repeated forms. The careful detailing is more the result of an underlying fundamental idea than of a costly ennobling of the material, an aspect that clearly differentiates Dutch architecture, which generally operates with restricted budgets, from Swiss Minimalism.

The above is applicable also to the Eurotwin Business Centre on Papaverweg in Amsterdam (1992–93), which was inserted like an ordering element in an indeterminate industrial zone. A pair of five-storey office buildings, each with an adjoining low-rise row of sheds, are placed as mirror images of each other. The buildings are clad with timber laths, which in the case of the office blocks are mounted vertically and interrupted by horizontal strip windows. The tensions in this ensemble of different sized boxes is not the result of the taut composition alone but is also created by the treatment of the facade materials: the way they change directions, the different colours, the contrast between shiny and matt, absorbing or reflecting light, open or closed. These various qualities produce a building that combines modesty and sophistication in a striking manner. ›

It was in minimal architecture that structures such as buildings to house rail transport technology (see the projects by Gigon/Guyer, Morger & Degelo and Herzog & de Meuron in this book) first became pieces of architecture that attracted the interest of critics and the public. The monolithic sculptures appeared to transfer Minimal Art to urban space. With their Switching Stations for PTT Telecom in Amsterdam (1995–97) Claus en Kaan approached a similar commission with a humour of their own, initially giving the sketch designs of their abstract boxes names such as "Reconstruction", "Amsterdam School" or "Classical City". The end product was two series of closed volumes with differently coloured or treated surfaces that enter into an individual relationship with the surroundings in which they are placed. ›

PTT Telecom Switching Stations, Amsterdam, The Netherlands 1995–97
The minimalist boxes for the Telecom glass fibre network are placed at different outdoor locations. Although they all follow a uniform concept each box has its own special characteristics that also reflect the context of its particular environment.

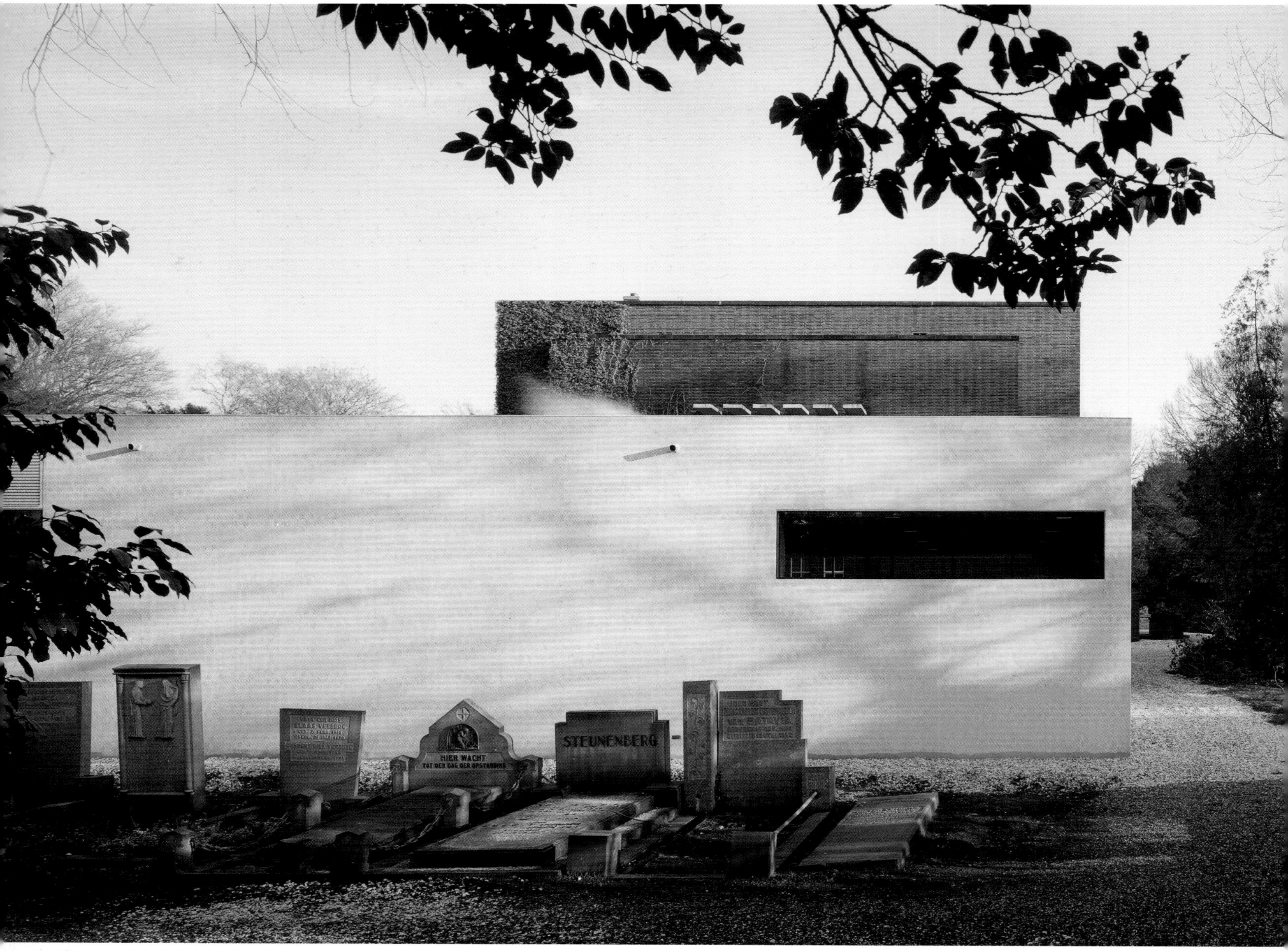

Reception Pavilion, Zorgvlied Cemetery, Amstelveen, The Netherlands 1995–98 The new reception pavilion inserts itself among the tombstones of the cemetery. The minimal use of the materials light grey stucco, glass and steel and the way the building is placed on ground covered with white gravel connect the condolence room with the cemetery on a single level thus creating a transition between inside and outside.

With the Reception Pavilion at Zorgvlied Cemetery in Amstelveen (1995–98) Claus en Kaan succeeded in making a carefully positioned piece of abstract architecture that, together with the cemetery's funeral hall, built in a conglomerate 1930s style, creates a special context. Their plain white building rises directly from the gravel-covered ground, its powerful roof projects towards the old building defining a new outdoor space between the two structures. The permeable glass front forms a subtle boundary between inside and outside. According to Hans Ibelings it was the architects' intention to create here an "invisible architecture" that can also be read as a "metaphor for absence" and yet with its positive atmosphere it can, in some way, balance the feeling of loss. At the same time this building, conceived with such reserve, emanates a great strength. ›

The same can be said of Claus en Kaan's recently opened Vught Concentration Camp Museum (2000–02). After decades the remains of the former concentration camp were finally converted into a memorial for which Michael van Gessel developed the landscape plan. Claus en Kaan designed the exhibition building along with the offices of the foundation, which stands at the entrance to the camp like a gate. The striking facade of the elongated building is made up of long thin strips of terracotta that alternate with broader, slightly recessed bands of rendered brickwork to create a striped effect. At the same time the economic use of incised window openings, which like in the Eurotwin Business Centre contrast with the facade in terms of material, colour and the different degrees of permeability, contributes to the building's expressive strength. The interior is an additive assembly of larger and smaller spaces that offers two routes, one for entering and one for leaving the building, thus giving visitors a series of different architectural impressions. □

Angeli Sachs

Vught Concentration Camp Museum, The Netherlands 2000–02 The remains of the Vught concentration camp erected by the Nazis lie in the shadow of a prison later erected in the former camp. The exhibition building marks the entrance to the camp and simultaneously reveals a view of it.

Vught Concentration Camp Museum, The Netherlands 2000–02
The sequence of spaces in the museum includes a memorial room with a ceiling opening most likely inspired by Karl Friedrich Schinkel's Neue Wache. In this space 750 plaques are mounted inscribed with the dates of birth and death of those who were incarcerated here.

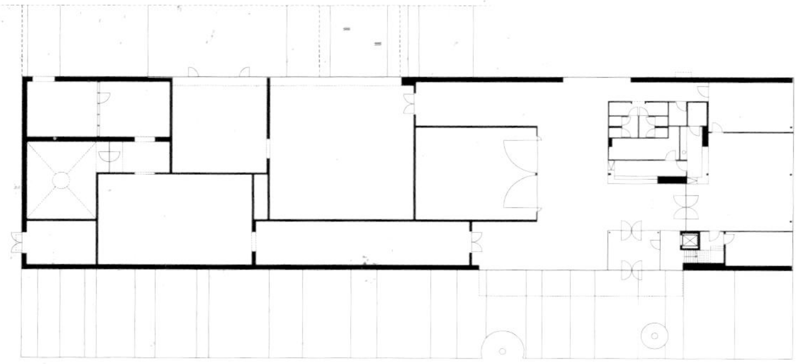

Adriaan J.W. Koopman
Elias Koopman
Rinse Koopmans
Hartog Koperberg
Ines Koperberg
Martinus I. Korpershoek
Eustachius A. Kortbeek

Dominique Perrault

Dominique Perrault explicitly emphasises his interest in Minimal Art. His preference for grid structures, industrial materials and geometric primary forms is clearly close to sculptures by artists such as Sol LeWitt, Donald Judd and Carl Andre. His criticism of narrative tendencies in architecture recalls the minimalist tradition of giving works the name "Untitled". His belief that architecture must, so to speak, be completed by its users is related to the minimalist idea of an aesthetic of participation.

However, in contrast to many of his colleagues, Perrault is not interested in the idea of reduction nor in any kind of authenticity of materials. He is far more concerned with reflecting the direct violent act of architectural intervention. In his case this is called "authority" or "physical reality". Minimal artists would have used the term "presence". And indeed his Technical Book Centre for Higher Education in Bussy-Saint-Georges, France (1993–95), positioned along the highway A4 and the suburban railway line A between Paris und Marne-la-Vallée achieves its greatest effect when the blocks suddenly materialise in front of the eyes of those travelling by. The additive use of cubes of different sizes, clad with aluminium panels and movable louvers and placed on the site without the use of a plinth, seems at first glance like a monumental enlargement of a minimalist sculpture. ›

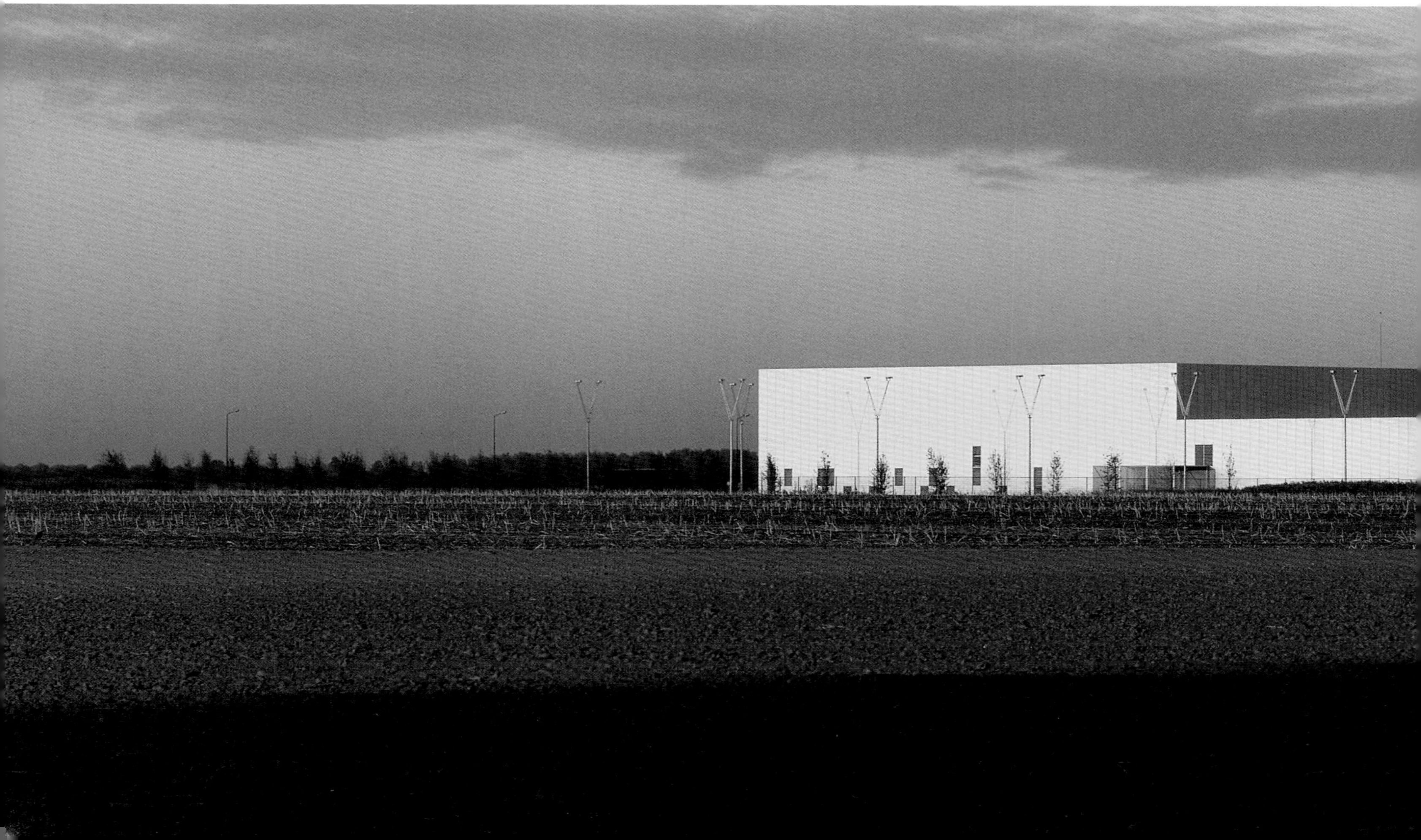

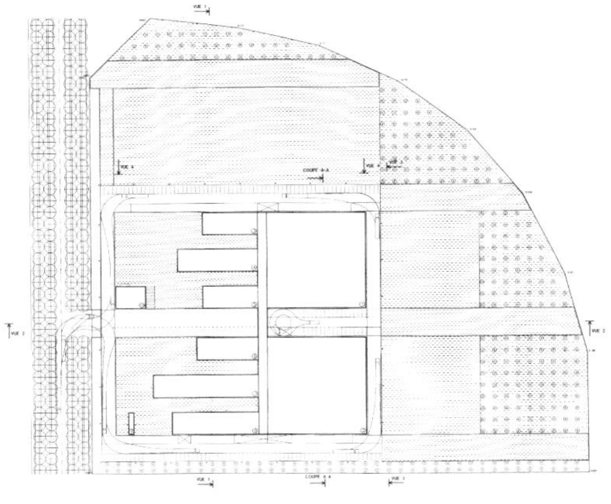

Technical Book Centre, Bussy-Saint-Georges, Paris, France
1993–95 The Technical Book Centre is used by the university libraries in the Paris region for the conservation of a part of their scientific collections. It also houses areas for the legal deposit of publications, for book repair, conference rooms and workshops. The central axis is a covered interior roadway. An expansion towards the north, south, and east is possible.

When Perrault emphasises that his primary interest lies in positioning buildings "between presence and disappearance" he touches on another crucial theme of Minimal Art—albeit one previously seldom theoretically analysed—i.e. the play with visual deception and revelation, with distortion and its correction and with *trompe-l'oeil*. His projects can be viewed as a productive development of minimalist principles and assist in arriving at a new reading of minimal art from a current, architectural perspective. Perrault's APLIX factory in Le Cellier-sur-Loire, Nantes (1997–99) achieves a similar effect as Donald Judd's sculptures in Marfa, Texas which fascinate the viewer by the way they seem to disappear into their surroundings only to emerge again. However, whereas in the case of Judd's work nature was the dominant reference, in Perrault's case there is no immovable point of reference but at best, a flexible mesh of relationships that alters over the course of time. This factory, a modular structure built on a "crossword puzzle grid", as he describes it, with facades of metal panels that like Fresnel lenses refract and reflect their surroundings does not need a spectacular landscape as a frame. It is not designed for a specific site; it neither follows a definite typology nor makes any clear reference to the site. On the contrary it embodies the complex facets of meaning characteristic of such constantly changing industrial buildings in surroundings that themselves continuously alter. What goes on inside remains mysterious. At the moment self-adherent fibre fabric and self-supporting systems are manufactured there. What these in fact are hardly anybody knows and what will go on there in three years time is in the stars. □

Philip Ursprung

APLIX Factory, Nantes, France 1997–99 The 7.7-meter-high facade is treated like a blind facade. The inside is organised around three interior garden patios. Only the tips of trees are visible when seen from a certain distance. The vaguely shining sheet metal on the facade lets the materiality of the factory blend into the surrounding landscape. "Nature" is evoked as a blurred image.

APLIX Factory, Nantes, France 1997–99 In order to allow for future expansion the project aims at maximum flexibility. It is based on a 20 × 20 metre grid. The factory is shaped in a long rectangle patterned by a series of setbacks. Its "backbone" is an interior roadway which runs parallel to the Route Nationale 23.

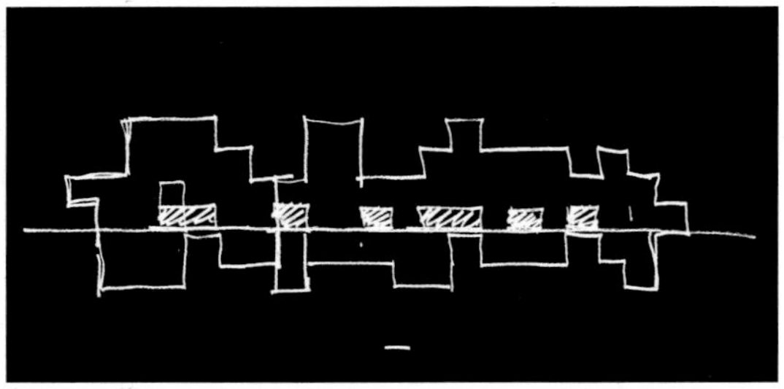

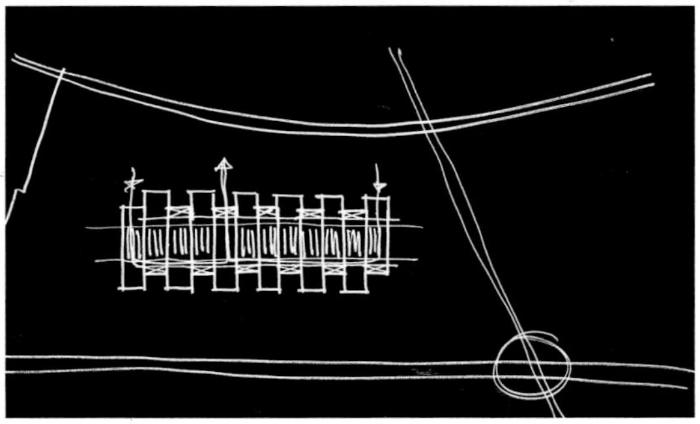

SANAA Kazuyo Sejima + Ryue Nishizawa

The Japanese architectural practice SANAA actually consists of three offices: Kazuyo Sejima's office, founded in 1987, the partnership she formed in 1995 with Ryue Nishizawa and Ryue Nishizawa's own office. Their projects seem highly aesthetic, lucid and reserved and they combine these qualities with a particular kind of modern urbanity. Toyo Ito calls Sejima "a new type of architect" describing her way of working, which she herself sees as "a continuous process of discovery", as "diagram architecture … She arranges the functional conditions which the building is expected to hold, in a final diagram of the space, then she immediately converts that scheme into reality." This is equally applicable to the choice of materials and colours, which are also essentially determined at the design stage. Everything is considered in advance and her architecture is therefore abstract and conceptual in a way reminiscent of Minimal or Conceptual Art.

An excellent example is the multifunctional Police Box at Chofu Station in Tokyo (1993–94), that combines its functions, namely maintaining law and order in a city suburb and providing rest areas and storage space, with the quality of a contemporary landmark. The striking narrow box stands in heterogeneous surroundings between the railway station and its forecourt. A cylindrical internal structure connects the block's two long walls and also stabilises both of them. The black external walls of polished stainless steel panels and the circular opening cut in the upper area make the Police Box an object that commands attention. The shiny black surface reflects its surroundings placing the box in a permanently changing relationship to the external world. ›

Police Box at Chofu Station, Tokyo, Japan 1993–94 The black building with shiny facade that reflects its surroundings integrates primary geometric forms that either emerge from the box or penetrate it as a hole and thus becomes a minimalist sculpture that allows a broad spectrum of ways to perceive it.

Pachinko Parlor III in Hitachiohta, Ibaraki (1995–96) is a gaming hall. Situated on the urban periphery along a highway and surrounded by faceless container buildings that differ from each other only in the signs attached to them, this building dedicated to the pleasures of gambling attracts attention to itself by transforming its colourful interior life into a seductive architectural image on the street facade. The floor plan of the rectangular box follows the system of the gaming machines arranged in rows. But the facade makes a slight curve inwards taking up the curve of the road and at the same time giving the building internally and externally a certain dynamic quality. ›

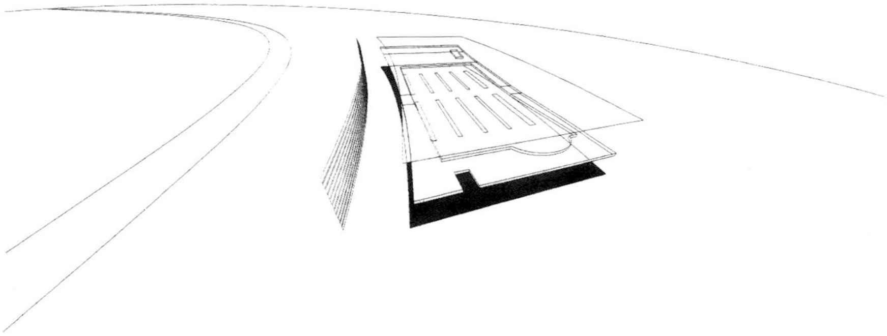

Pachinko Parlor III, Hitachiohta, Ibaraki, Japan 1995–96 The colour concept used for both the interior and the facade of the Pachinko Parlour responds to the building's dynamic quality and emphasises the virtual world of the gaming machines.

Whereas Kazuyo Sejima's interest originally lay more in the relationship between what she described as "action and its field", the focal point of her work has shifted in later projects to the phenomenon of the "boundary": "I am now trying to think about many kinds of boundary at once, and not only physical ones such as between rooms or spaces, between inside or outside. But I think have always been interested in how to make the plan, which also means how to make the boundary."

In the Park Café in Koga, Ibaraki prefecture (1996–98) the boundaries between inside and outside and between the spaces in the interior seem to have been almost entirely eliminated, a fact underlined by the extreme thinness of the structural members. The roof is a steel sheet only 25 mm thick and each of the 100 steel supports has a diameter of 60.5 mm. The architect's truly minimalist concept aims at avoiding placing an object in the extensive landscaped park instead inserting a construction which itself appears to be part of nature. According to the season sliding glass doors allow a changing definition of inside and outside space, the shiny surfaces to the tables reflect the vegetation and the skies and multiply the real images of nature to create a complex virtual experience. ›

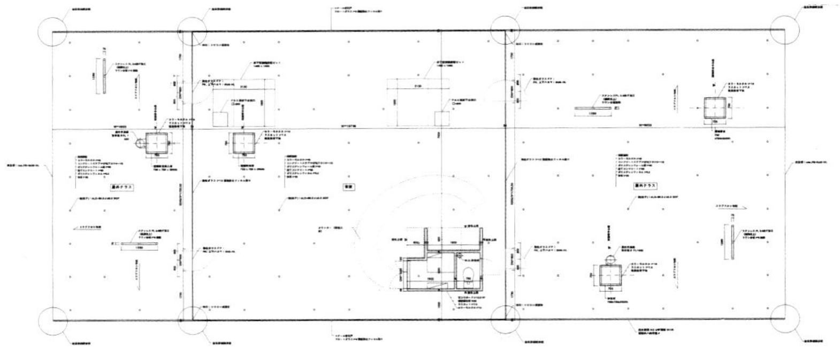

Park Café, Koga, Ibaraki, Japan 1996–98 The lightness of the forest of columns and of the roof they carry emphasises the flowing transition between inside and outside and allows this pavilion-like building to become almost a part of nature.

CASA-S in Okayama (1997) is a translucent cube to which the criteria of introversion described earlier appear to apply. The facade has few openings and is articulated by the uprights of the substructure that supports the cladding and by the latter's horizontal corrugations. It seems to function as a communication filter, which, especially when the building is fully lit-up, offers passers-by a schematic indication of what goes on inside. Between the facade and the inward-facing rooms of this house for three generations of a family is a double-height corridor, which functions as a semi-public area. One requirement of the brief was to achieve a balance between creating a feeling of community and the requirement of each family member for a space of their own. The communal dining and living room for the family are on the upper floor; the various private spaces are on the ground floor. Wooden folding doors and mobile louvers allow the interior layout to be altered whenever required, the spaces can be connected or separated in a variety of ways. □

Angeli Sachs

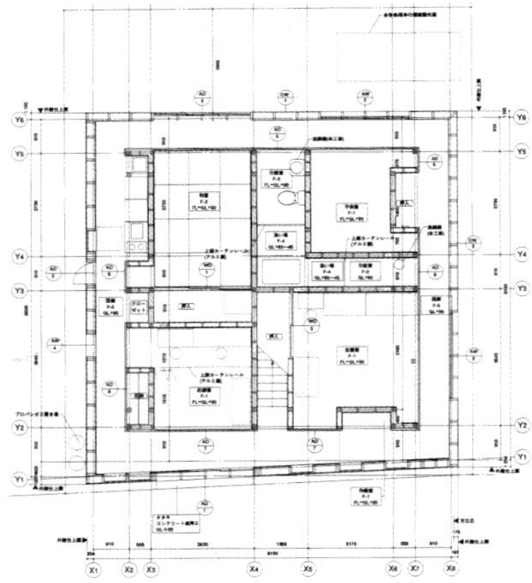

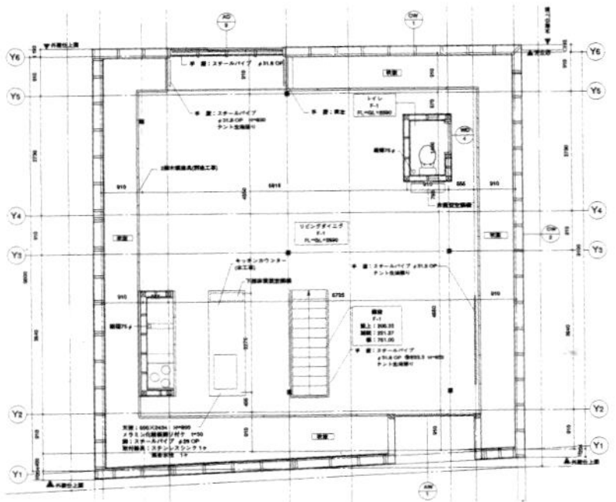

CASA-S, Okayama, Japan 1997 The minimalist appearance of the interior is in fact based on a highly complex concept that offers the inhabitants every imaginable possibility of adapting their spatial situation to meet their momentary needs.

BeL

At first gaze this project appears to possess all those qualities that together make up the canon of minimalism: immaculate surfaces, a regular geometry and rigorously reduced pieces of furniture surrounded by a sublime emptiness. Its use as a trade-fair stand refers to one of architectural minimalism's central cultural functions: the creation of atmospheric backgrounds for the presentation of fetish objects. Utterly white walls intensify antiseptically clean light from a ceiling of fluorescent tubes and appear to be fully absorbed in a blissful universe of London Minimalism. Or perhaps not? There is something unsettling about this merciless purism; the perfection of its appearance shifts the space into another realm, giving it the artificiality of a computer rendering.

Yet this illusion exists only as long as the space is free of human beings. When it is actually used, unexpected ambiguities crop up that disturb the well-staged illusion. The furniture, which seemed so perfectly matched to the image, suddenly appears somewhat too small, making people sitting on it look like adults that have strayed into a children's room. Even the act of sitting down itself is unsettling. In contrast to the expectations awakened by the sharp-edged geometry of the furniture the chairs and tables are in fact made of soft foam rubber. This unexpected comfort begins to distort the self-image that this space conveys. Instead of perpetuating the minimalist ideal image of a perfect world the architects expose the fragility of the order on which this world is based. This space opens up an area of tension in which the promise made by the norm is engaged in permanent conflict with its own arbitrariness. ›

DIN, Hanover Fair, Germany 2002 Developed as a stand to circulate on industrial fairs for a duration of four years, this fair actually carefully circumvents the rhetoric of its typology. With its hybrid atmosphere half-way between art gallery, stage set and bar lounge, it provides a spatial framework which—instead of simply featuring the displayed products—both celebrates and questions their intrinsic design values.

DIN

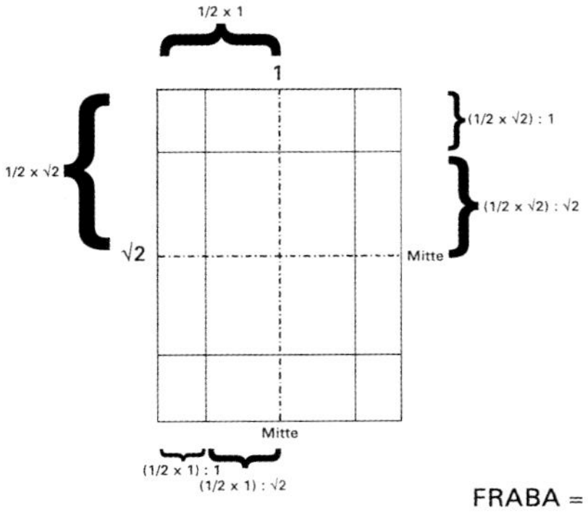
1/2 x 1
1
(1/2 x √2) : 1
1/2 x √2
(1/2 x √2) : √2
√2
Mitte
Mitte
(1/2 x 1) : 1
(1/2 x 1) : √2

FRABA = 1: √2

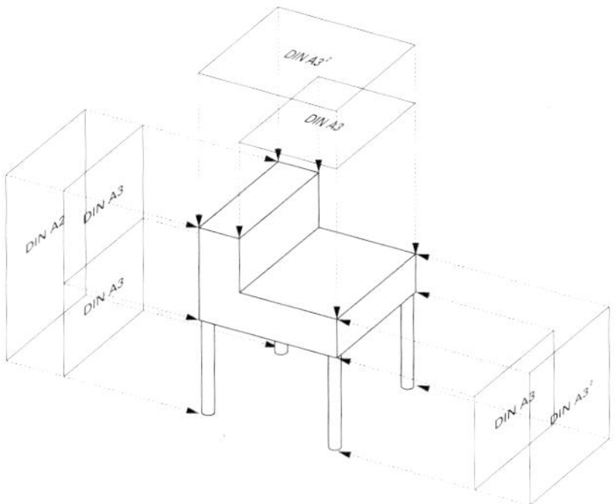
DIN A2
DIN A3
DIN A3
DIN A3
DIN A3

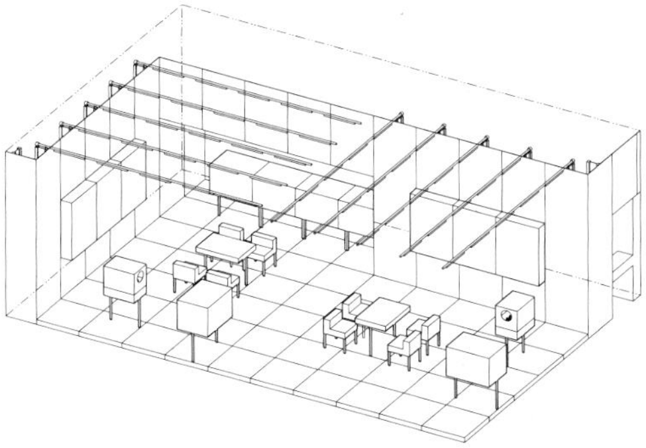

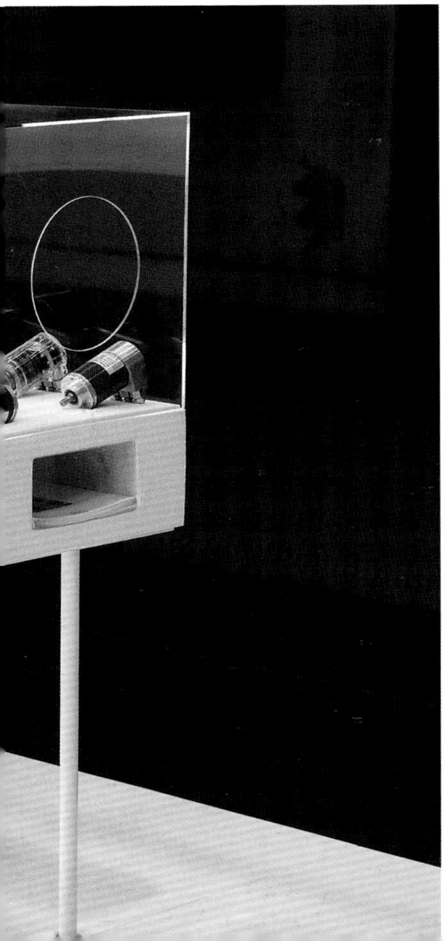

This norm makes its concrete appearance here in the guise of the DIN format, founded by the Deutsche Industrie-Norm. In response to the fact that the corporate identity of the company exhibiting here (a manufacturer of precision instruments) is entirely based on this ordering system the architects laid a DIN modular grid over the entire stand. Every object had to be integrated in this system, therefore the chairs and tables had to be either larger or smaller than usual. The architects opted for a reduction in size—the chairs, for example, are A3.

You do not immediately notice this irritation in terms of scale as the entire system is harmonious, resolved within itself, but at the very latest when heavyweight managers lower their massive bodies onto the delicate chairs, the comic aspect of this scenario is unleashed. The demystification of the "reduced space", which means everything to architectural minimalism, here follows precisely the same theatrical logic with which minimal artists present their sculptures. As is the case with such artists, BeL are also not interested in emptying space but in continuously charging it with the opposite of itself. □

Ilka & Andreas Ruby

DIN, Hanover Fair, Germany 2002 Unspeakably tainted with the eerie presence of a De Chirico landscape cross-bred with a David Lynch interior, the space is nevertheless made of real materials: the walls and ground consist of solid surface material which is mineral-based and very rigid. However, the furniture and display socles are made of polyurethane foam whose soft consistency is well-disguised in the hard-edge allure of its cubic forms.

FRABA
POSITAL
POSITAL
ABSOLUTE POSITION
Intelligente Winkelcodierer
und Neigungssensoren:
Integrierte Funktionalität
entlastet die Steuerung
www.posital.de

OMA Office for Metropolitan Architecture I

The Guggenheim Hermitage is the unusual product of collaboration between the Guggenheim Foundation and the St. Petersburg Hermitage, in which the two museums exchange, for a certain period of time, selected works from their respective collections. Particularly for the historic museum in St. Petersburg the project was intended to establish the flow of capital urgently required for the maintenance of its exhibition buildings. Whereas these buildings offered ample space to exhibit the Guggenheim works, the Guggenheim Foundation had first of all to find a suitable place to show the Hermitage paintings which they eventually found in, of all places, the cathedral of American capitalism —Las Vegas. And in order to display the art treasures of the former Soviet empire to as large a public as possible the exhibition was not housed in a building of its own but in one of Las Vegas' largest mega-resorts—The Venetian: a combination of casino, hotel, retail shopping and restaurants, housed in a recreation of famous urban spaces in Venice that is as surreal as it is naturalistic.

To accomplish the task of making a space for exhibiting art in a place that is itself nothing other than one giant show, the Office for Metropolitan Architecture was selected, clearly with the hope that Rem Koolhaas was best suited to solving this awkward alliance of art and commerce in a sovereign fashion. Given these expectations the project he came up with was all the more surprising: amazingly in Las Vegas the protagonist of Dirty Realism and master of the calculated provocation went into hiding and disguised himself with the cultivated reserve displayed by an introverted museum box that appears to be entirely inspired by the obsessive reduction of Essential Minimalism: a windowless cubic interior—its horizontal surfaces clad in wood, the vertical ones lined in steel—that stretches the minimalist elimination of details to the limit. Instead of picture hooks or cords each painting is mounted on the walls by magnets attached to the back, which also serve as protection against theft.

But this minimalist liaison comes to an abrupt end once the surrounding space makes itself noticeable. The apparent autonomy of the space dissolves like a mirage; left behind is a project that in fact relates to its context in every respect. ›

Guggenheim Hermitage, Las Vegas, Nevada, USA 2001 Integrated in one of the new mega resorts of Las Vegas, the Guggenheim Hermitage is a rare timeout for the eye and mind within the neon-fed frenzyness of Americas gaming polis. Exposing just one of its walls to the outside, the gallery keeps a low profile within the hyper-real pastiche of Venice enveloping a veritable armada of shops, restaurants and casino facilities. These politics of hiding seem to grant the project a steady presence, contrary to its twin next door—the Guggenheim Museum Las Vegas—which had to close its doors within just 15 months of opening (its 2,000 daily visitors being only half of what their business plan had projected).

This starts with the materials of the gallery walls: instead of smooth concrete or noble natural stone they are made of Corten steel—a material one could hardly describe as noble as it ultimately exposes the arrested state of its own decay (corrosion). Thanks to its special chemical composition it offers greater resistance to atmospheric corrosion than other steels. As it weathers it forms a layer of rust that subsequently provides a protective coating against further corrosion. That is to say it is essentially a material for external use and when Koolhaas employs it here in the interior of the building then his aim is to metaphorically link the building's air-conditioned interiority with external space once again.

This movement towards the outside is assisted by a glazed slit running along the gallery wall like a transparent skirting board, which allows a glimpse of the artificial marble of the shopping passages behind in The Venetian. In this way Koolhaas undermines the introversion of space always pursued in Essential Minimalism and in the process creates a contact with the context that is minimal, but for that reason all the more effective. In contrast to the white cube of Modernism, which always isolates art from its social surrounding, this "brown cube" operates with the value system that prevails in its immediate environment. Koolhaas makes it into the real casino safe in the sense that the art collection exhibited inside it is probably the most valuable thing the building has to offer. □

Ilka & Andreas Ruby

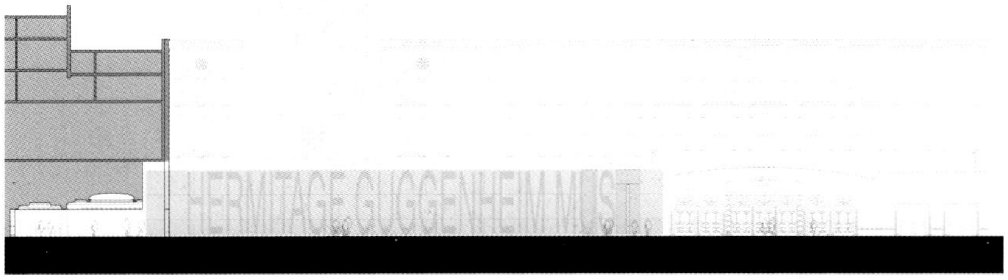

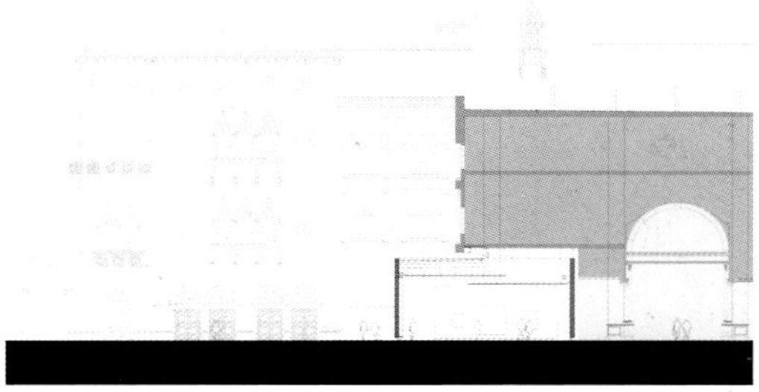

Projects III If Essential Minimalism results from a take-over of Minimal Art's look by transposing the reductionist aesthetic of Modernism's "less is more" and propelling it into the stylish apotheosis of a "least is most", and if, furthermore, Meta-Minimalism arises from the fact that a number of architects—previously unconnected with Minimalist Architecture—decide to appropriate the latter's formal language while cultivating it for their own aims, then Trans-minimalism is a theoretical speculation about an architecture which would allow itself to be inspired not by the forms but by the concepts of Minimal Art.

For it is a fact that the formal vocabulary of Minimal Art—taking sculpture down from its pedestal, repetition instead of composition, primary geometry with complex effects on our perception, smooth surfaces without detail—was for its protagonists not an end in itself but rather a means of discovering a new "inclusive" space they wished to produce by dissolving the boundaries around the artwork and allowing it to expand into the surrounding space.

To this end they produced objects that, due to their abstraction, offer the gaze nothing to fix on but reflect it back directly into the surrounding space thus tending to dissolve the boundary between art and non-art, between figure and ground.

Applied 1:1 to architecture and interpreted as a "building manual" these principles paradoxically produce precisely the opposite effect, i.e. they renew and heighten the distinction between the object and its surroundings. The reason for this difference with all its implications most probably lies in the difference between the systems of architecture and art. Whereas the social experience of minimalist art ultimately takes place in the space around it, architecture's social experience occurs to a major extent in the interior of buildings. Therefore the dissolution of spatial boundaries that is effected in Minimal Art by activating the space around the sculpture, should in architecture logically include the interior of the building also. The reflection of the viewer's gaze from the surface of the minimalist artwork back into the surrounding space ought in a (trans-minimalist) architecture to transform into a transition of the architectural boundary between external and internal space. To achieve this transitional quality architecture must inevitably abandon the formal canon derived from Minimal Art and instead look for architectural processes that place the building in a relationship with its context by creating overlaps between its interior and exterior spaces on the level of material, structure, programme, topography and typology.

Ilka & Andreas Ruby

eru Ban

In the eyes of those conditioned by *Wallpaper** the work of Shigeru Ban must look like the ultimate incarnation of minimalist architecture, after all here reduction appears to penetrate to the very bones of architecture. However Ban is excluded from the long-running cultivated dispute between Ando, Pawson, etc. as to whose walls are the smoothest for the simple reason that his houses often have no walls at all. Taking the Modernist metaphor of the curtain wall quite literally, in his Curtain Wall House in Itabashi-ku, Tokyo (1995) he makes the facade from a piece of material. By drawing this curtain the inhabitant can determine whether the act of living is to be conducted inside the boundaries of his townhouse or to become part of public street life in the neighbourhood. Sliding glass doors running behind the curtain provide the climatic protection necessary in winter. ›

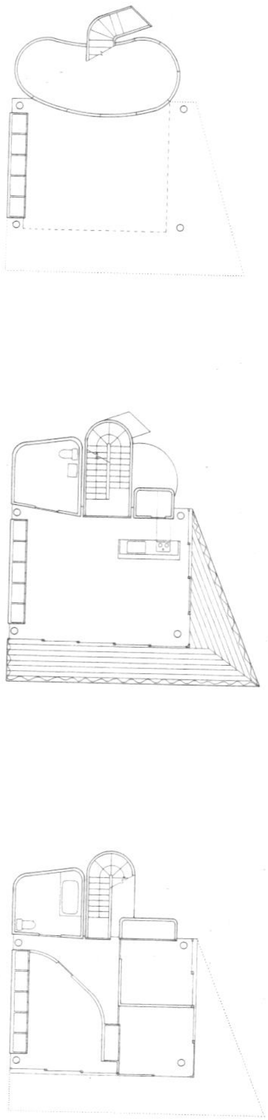

Curtain Wall House, Itabashi-ku, Tokyo, Japan 1995 Conceived like a body enveloped by a subsequent garment layer, this house actually has two facades: the exposed curtain that provides visual intimacy when closed; and a recessed screen of fully-transparent sliding doors granting protection against outside noise and weather.

The Wall-Less House in Karuizawa, Kitasaku-Gun, Nagano (1997) consists of a floor and a roof slab only. It is completely open at the sides so that interior space flows without interruption into the natural surroundings of the site. Transparent sliding doors concealed in the wall against the slope—the only wall in fact—here again provide minimum protection against the elements. Instead of fixed internal walls the house has a system of sliding wooden partitions that can, when required, be used to divide the open space into living room, bedroom and bathroom and when not needed can be slid away to one side. ›

Wall-Less House, Karuizawa, Nagano, Japan 1997 This summer residence project almost seems like the antithesis of a house, consisting solely of a ground slab and a roof which literally seem to be rammed into the earth of the building's mountain site. Consequently the living space of the house totally expands into its natural surroundings, appropriating its views as its airy wallpaper.

In the Naked House in Kawagoe-shi (2002) five members of a family bridging several different generations live in space-boxes mounted on castors. These boxes can be freely positioned in the long hall of the house, which is lit through translucent facades, and can either stand separately or be connected to form long "tubes".

But to read his work as the expression of a progressive subtraction of architectural material would miss the point of Shigeru Ban's volatile spatial dispositions. Including it in the reductionist eschatology that characterises architectural minimalism of the European kind would merely repeat that misunderstanding with which the representatives of minimalist art were once confronted. The reductionist reading of their work retroactively inserted into it elements, which, it was thought, had been subtracted but which in fact—as Philip Ursprung has explained in his introductory essay to this book—the authors of these works had never imagined in the first place. In precisely the same sense nothing is subtracted from Ban's spaces. Instead, quite simply, nothing is added that, from the European perspective, might be regarded as necessary—for example walls. In traditional Japanese domestic architecture, to which Ban refers, there are no private spaces. A single space served as dining, working, living and sleeping area. Equally foreign to this culture is the idea of closed external walls in the sense of brick or masonry facades. Instead the open timber structure is screened from the outside by wooden frames spanned with rice paper. The "emptiness" in Shigeru Ban's architecture is therefore not the outcome of a striving for reduction but reveals an understanding of material whose cultural codes do not match the values of the Western tradition, often assumed to be universal.

Instead of working on a reductionist project Shigeru Ban conducts a permanent mutation of architecture's constituent elements such as walls, doors, windows and fittings. The further development of the Japanese architectural tradition plays an important role in this process. For example Ban replaces wood with less expensive cardboard tubes (which have a similar load-bearing capacity to wood and can be made water- and fire-resistant through the use of special techniques). ›

Naked House, Tokyo, Japan 2000 Seemingly closed to the outside, this hangar-like space of the five-person house is generously filled with daylight filtered through its multi-layered facades. Instead of conventional room partitions, the interior features spatial boxes put on castors which can be used as separate units, or grouped together to form collective enclosures.

His research into materials enabled Ban to develop, in the shortest time possible, Minimal Shelters for those left homeless by the earthquake in Kobe in 1995. He subsequently used this material on a regular basis as a substitute for conventional steel, concrete or timber structural systems. Furthermore the facade of the Naked House, through which light pours, is not another example of that translucence with which European Minimalism believes it can outdistance Modernism (and its cult of transparency). On the contrary, Ban is concerned here with achieving a contemporary interpretation of the traditional Shoij window. He therefore enclosed the steel structure of the house with a double facade that externally carries plastic panels reinforced with glass fibres and internally is spanned with lengths of nylon. In the cavity between the facade layers he placed plastic bags filled with polyethylene threads that ensure adequate thermal insulation and give the interior precisely that subdued daylight so characteristic of traditional Japanese houses. □

Ilka & Andreas Ruby

Miyake Design Studio Gallery, Shiwuya-ku, Tokyo, Japan 1994
After having worked with paper tubes as display structures for exhibitions, Ban discovered that paper tubes are strong enough to serve as construction material of architecture in its own right. Entirely prefabricated and assembled on site, the paper tube structure allows for an "instant architecture" able to appear and disappear like the temporary feast architectures of the cherry blossom garden parties so popular in Japan.

OMA Office for Metropolitan Architecture II

The Italian fashion house Prada is one of the designer labels whose success story is most intimately linked with the heyday of Essential Minimalism. In the space of just a few years Prada had opened more than 200 outlets worldwide, all of them characterised by the same minimalist principles: empty spaces with long shelves in pale green (the Prada colour) on which a limited number of shoes and items of clothing, indirectly lit by neon light, were effectively placed. But at the end of the 1990s, when minimalism inflated to become the ubiquitous design paradigm of brand name consumerism, Prada saw the need to change direction in order to re-establish the exclusivity of its brand. When the company contacted Rem Koolhaas and his Office for Metropolitan Architecture to build a new epicenter (a kind of flagship store with the special function of defining the brand name) this was, in fact, a discreet commission to give Prada a post-minimalist look. This project was lent additional spice by the fact that the store was to be opened in the Soho district of New York, which, having been gentrified by the lifestyle industry, in the 1990s was the high altar of "boutique Cistercianism" (Charles Jencks). Openly dismissive of the crypto-spiritual reduction characteristic of minimalist shop design, Koolhaas used this opportunity to lead this creed's holy cows to the slaughterhouse, one after another. He responded to the minimalist commandment regarding the reduction of materials with a veritable cacophony of different surfaces and finishes, deliberately combining expensive natural materials with cheap industrial products (for instance the solid wood flooring on the entrance level that directly abuts the display window back wall made of polycarbonate sandwich panels). On the lower ground floor Koolhaas applies an everyday aesthetic familiar from suburban shopping centres which Pawson, Silvestrin & Co. did their utmost to keep at bay from their ethereal chapels of consumption: suspended

Prada Epicenter Store, New York, USA 2001 Through an assortment of materials applied all over the space, Koolhaas overcharges the atmosphere in order to deny the sold product its aura. Enshrined in metal boxes which suspiciously resemble the golden cages for go-go dancers in night clubs, the displayed clothes have a rather ambiguous presence. As the cages are fixed to tracks in the ceiling, they can be pushed to the end of the space in order to make room for cultural events in the evenings.

ceilings made of reflective stainless steel sheeting, floor covering with a monstrous black and white checkerboard pattern and, here and there, bare plasterboard walls with rudimentarily skimmed joints.

Above all however Koolhaas tilted the logic of the minimalist display of goods through 180 degrees: whereas in the minimalist approach the architecture is always only an expensively refined and reduced background for the goods in the foreground Koolhaas makes the architecture a rough foreground which means that the goods automatically retire to the background. He does not even draw the line at the most sacred Prada dispositive, the pale green shelving, whose quality as a cult icon is unmistakeably expressed in Andreas Gursky's photographic works *Prada I* and *Prada II* (1997). Although keeping the shelving as a topos he deprives it of its aesthetic exclusivity by using it in a shelving system that runs on tracks—normally found in archives—which allows shelves, when not required, to be slid together in a space-saving way.

This mutation from shrine to archive transforms the product from a cult exhibition piece back to a useful object. This method of objectifying the exclusive is also propagated by the way goods are displayed on the ground floor: expanded metal cages hung from the ceiling, which can be moved through the space along tracks, are reminiscent of the transport logistics employed in manufacturing industry. In contrast to the presentation philosophy of earlier Prada boutiques, which was based on rarity, these mesh cages are stuffed with shoes and clothes which tends to emphasise more their concrete useful value (a leather bag) rather than any idealised value (an expensive piece of [brand] identity).

However Koolhaas does not confine his subversive transformation of brand consumerism to the level of shop display but extends it to the typology of the boutique as such. In contrast to shop design as practiced in Essential Minimalism where, to achieve its autonomy, the sales space is screened off from the outside, Koolhaas demonstratively opens it up again to society. Avoiding the symbolic gesture of transparency he instead alters the programming of the space during the course of 24 hours. After shop closing time the sales area becomes a culture area. The floor "wave" connecting the entrance level and the sales space on the lower ground floor opens up to reveal a small stage for public events such as intimate concerts, discussions and readings. Similarly the Prada shoes, during opening hours arranged in rows presented on broad steps opposite the "wave", make way in the evening for the public attending these events that uses the steps as an auditorium. The cages populating the air space can be shunted to the rear of the boutique to form a compact bunch. As a result of these measures New York's cultural life can temporarily penetrate the chambers of consumerism. The boundary between inside and outside, commercial and non-commercial becomes, for a time, permeable because Koolhaas refuses to recognise the primacy of the product but obliges consumption to share its aura with culture. □

Ilka & Andreas Ruby

Prada Epicenter Store, New York, USA 2001 To evade the admonition of constructing another temple of consumerism, Rem Koolhaas pushed the notion of a boutique well over its limits. A shop for expensive clothing during the day mutates into a space for cultural events after hours. To this end, a small stage integrated into the wave of the ground floor opens out and transforms the steps—normally used as shoe displays—into a seating area for the evening's events.

R&Sie...

The French architects R&Sie... (in French their name sounds like hérésie = heresy in English) apply the principle of minimising to an area that has, noticeably, hitherto remained untouched by the concentrated reductionist attack waged by the forces of minimalist architecture, i.e. the relationship between a building and its context. Whereas, generally speaking, the minimalist building expresses itself as an object detached from its surroundings R&Sie...'s interest lies precisely in undermining this traditional contrast between figure and ground. In their interventions the object disappears into the context, so to speak, by allowing itself to be infiltrated by the latter. Instead of asserting its importance like a piece of sculpture the architecture works as a kind of framework for perception, giving its location a more specific presence.

R&Sie... offer a demonstration of how this elimination of the object's isolation can be achieved in their "Maison Barak", Sommières, France (2001). Particularly interesting here is the conceptual metamorphosis between design and construction phases. In the original concept, instead of simply placing the house as an object on the site, the architects planned to re-model the existing topography, sliding the house into a newly created niche in the earth and then covering it over by continuing the ground. But in view of the tight budget available for this 180-square-metre building R&Sie... eventually decided not to fuse place and object literally but instead to interpret them conceptually as a single unit. To this end volumes that had, at an earlier design stage, been continuous were separated to produce a recumbent concrete cube and an aluminium tent frame propped against it. The soft form of the tent allows it to trace the change in level of the sloping site and also to make the rigid geometry of the house-box a part of the landscape. Both volumes are wrapped in a skin of green polyurethane sheeting that ultimately reconciles their volumetric differences and allows the house to disappear into its natural surroundings. ›

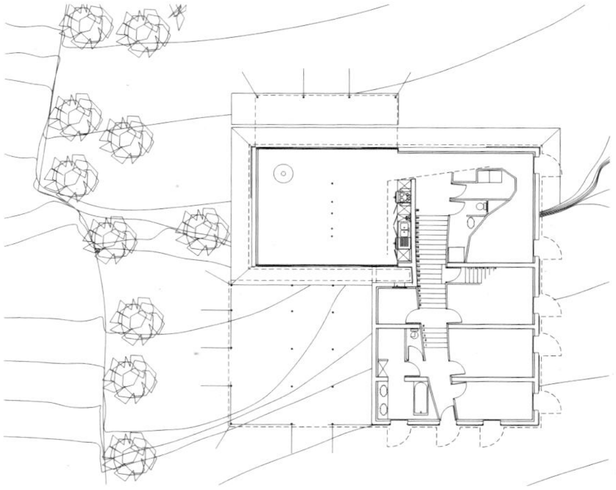

Barak House, Sommières, France 2001 Situated amidst the 500-metre *banmile* of a historical chateau in southern France where no new construction is allowed, the Barak house blends with its environment to pass for something other than architecture. As such, the house consists of a box-like volume comprising living and bedrooms, and an adjacent tent construction which for the time being serves as a playing area for children while bearing the potential to be "fully" built in the future as well.

However, R&Sie...'s interest in meshing their own interventions with the existing situation is not restricted to the visual appearance of the location but also extends to its material nature. In their Aqua Alta project for an extension to a school of architecture in Venice, Italy (1998, not carried out) they planned to lead the water from the lagoon city, unfiltered, into the building, allowing it to flow in canals through the various storeys and to rise upwards through transparent wall panels. They thus reworked the existing architectural context making it the flesh and blood of the building. In Silverrelief in Bangkok, Thailand (2002, in planning), their competition-winning design for a museum for contemporary art, they encase the exhibition building in a free-form shell of electrostatically-charged aluminium panels that attracts a second skin of dust particles drawn from the heavily polluted air of the Thai capital. The facade is not utilised to emphasise the art museum's independence of its surroundings but instead works as a contact surface that establishes a dialogue between the abstract space of the museum and the concrete situation of the site. The fact that the nakedness of the white cube exhibition halls should be clothed by, of all things, a thick layer of dust, means that their minimalist, purist rhetoric is continually contaminated by the conditions of the site. □

Ilka & Andreas Ruby

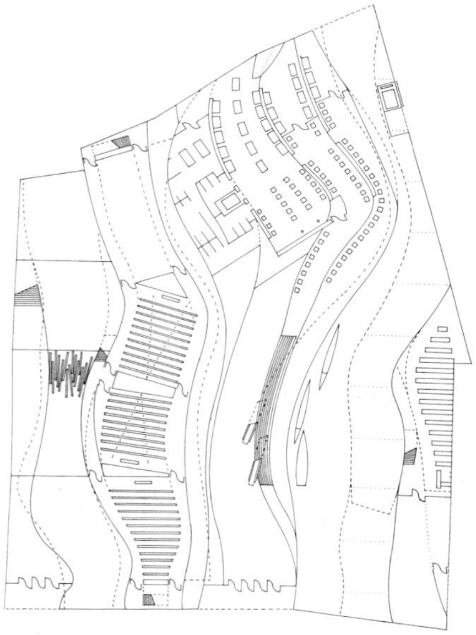

Aqua Alta, Extension to the Architecture School of Venice (project), Italy 1998
To insert itself as seamlessly as possible into its context, the new building literally borrows the predominant matter of the site. It leads the water of the lagoon into the building and lets it ascend through double-layered walls made of transparent plastic foil.

Bovolo

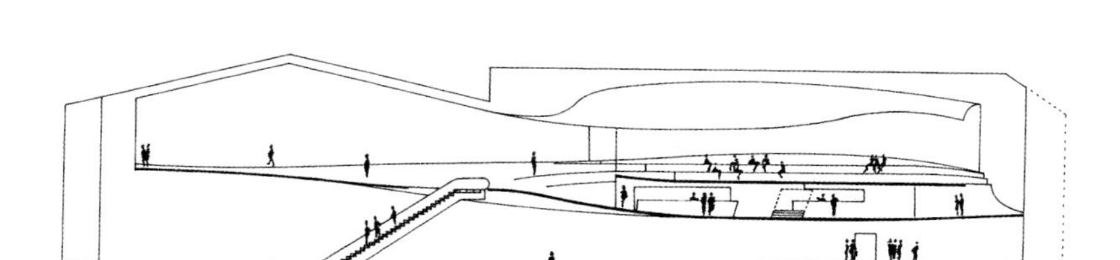

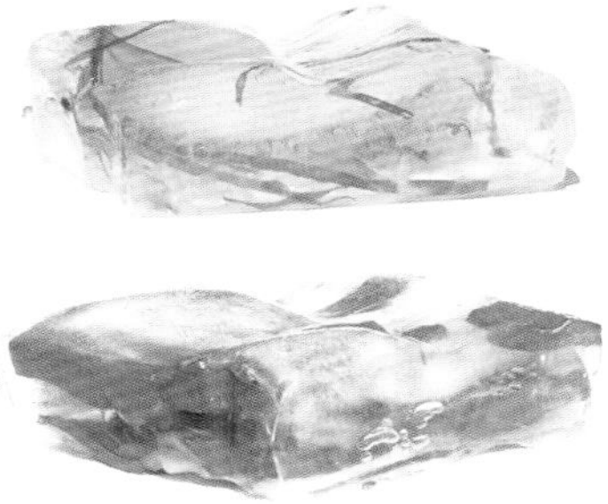

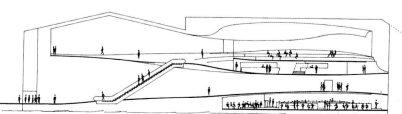

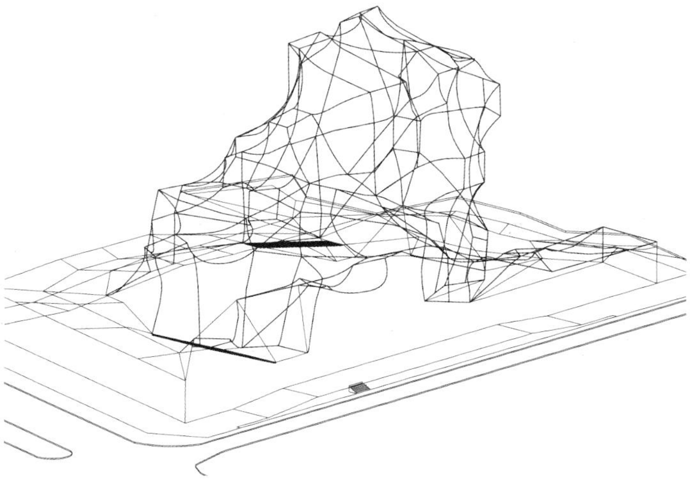

Silverrelief / B-mu, Bangkok, Thailand 2002 R&Sie... chose to make the dust-filled air of Bangkok—one of the most polluted cities in the world—the construction material for their planned art museum. With its facade out of electrostatically-charged aluminium, the building attracts the dust particles out of the air and accumulates a (truly site-specific) second skin. The interior gallery spaces, on the other hand, are furnished according to the purist aesthetic of the white cube, as if to ignore the counterfactual reality of the outside world.

Social Housing, Mulhouse, France 2002 In the tradition of Californian Case Study House Architecture, Lacaton & Vassal experiment with construction systems which until now have not been used in domestic architecture. For this social housing project they use a greenhouse construction system which can be adapted for domestic purposes while costing of only a fraction of conventional building material. What is saved in construction expenses, the architects invest in enlarging the affordable living area—which in this case is two to three times bigger than most social housing types.

With their architecture Lacaton & Vassal search for a simplicity that is neither an aesthetic attitude nor an ideological programme but which favours what is necessary, evident and obvious. In their view architecture should add to a situation only what it needs to function properly. Their interventions follow a logic based on efficiency: achieving maximum impact with minimum effort. The minimalist mainstream operates, for the most part, in completely the opposite way: investing an enormous amount of effort to create the impression of very little. To compensate for the emptiness of the space which thus ensues, essential minimalism directs its attention to the sublimation of the material. In contrast Lacaton & Vassal are interested primarily in space but in the sense of spatial extension rather than sculptural form. They therefore attack that minimalisation of space which derived from the doctrine of the "apartment for the minimum existence" (Wohnung für das Existenzminimum) expounded at the second CIAM-Congress in Frankfurt in 1929 and institutionalised after the Second World War in innumerable state housing programmes. Since that era the amount of space available has been increasingly considered a function of the existing budget, i.e. minimal budget = minimal space. Lacaton & Vassal rewrite this simplistic equation ad absurdum by creating the maximum amount of space with a minimum budget. ›

Social Housing, Mulhouse, France 2002 As the section shows, the ground floor is built in a standard concrete structure (also see image on the left) with a greenhouse construction sitting on top and effectively housing the rooms on the first floor (image on the right). Each unit has a small and a wide strip of space (alternatingly placed on the ground and first floor) as well as two outdoor spaces: a garden in front of the house and a roof terrace under the greenhouse roof (which can partially be opened to the sky).

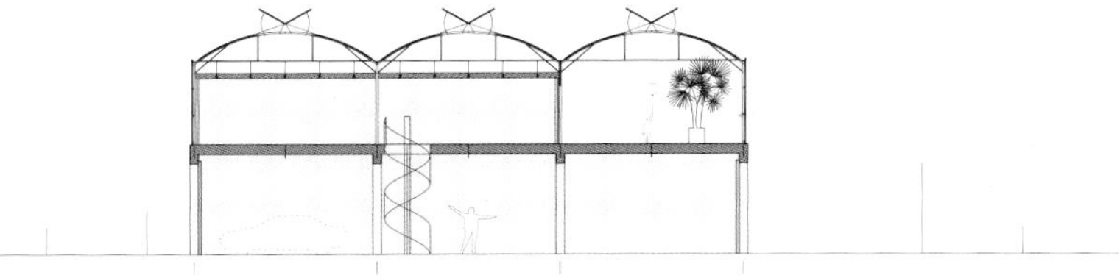

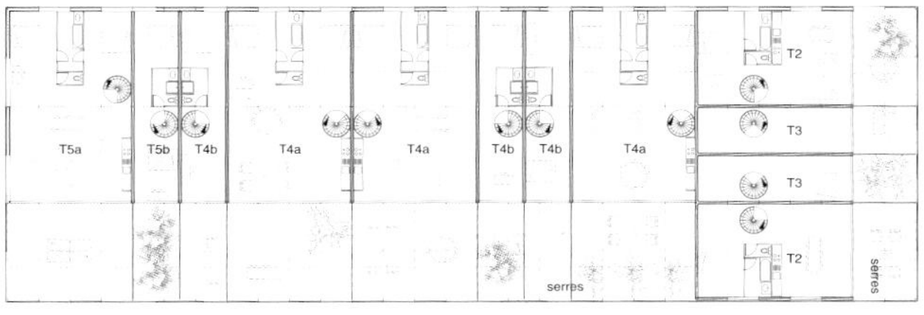

To achieve this end they work with unusually economical building materials and construction techniques that radically minimise the building's cost per square metre. What they save in the process they invest in increasing the floor area of the house. Employing this tactic in their Maison à Coutras they were able to provide 300 square metres of living space for a budget that, using conventional building methods, would have sufficed for about 100 square metres. This miraculous multiplication of space was achieved thanks to a standard greenhouse construction originally developed for large-scale use in intensive agriculture to cover areas of several thousand square metres and therefore considerably less expensive than "normal" architecture. (Simple adaptations modify the system to suit housing requirements).

In their recent Ilôt Schoettle project Lacaton & Vassal have applied this single-family house type to the design of a terraced housing estate. Although planned as a social housing scheme the floor area of the houses is two to three times greater than usual. The architects respond to the behaviourist conditioning imposed by the floor plans of state subsidised housing with open living plateaus extending over two storeys. Whereas the ground floors are concrete-built in the standard manner, the upper floors are glasshouses built according to the principle already demonstrated in Coutras. Consequently each house has two adjacent outdoor spaces: a front garden at ground floor level and on the first floor a winter garden that opens onto a terrace.

Lacaton & Vassal also provided spatial luxury using minimal means in their adaptation of the Palais de Tokyo. As the result of an abandoned conversion project this 1937 museum building had fallen into ruin. To transform it into an exhibition centre for contemporary art the architects restricted themselves to the necessary renovation measures (roof, structure, floors, electricity, lighting). They argued that the space was then architecturally complete and declared the enormous complex a museum space without colonising its atmosphere, reminiscent of industrial loft buildings in New York in the 1970s, with the insignia of the White Cube.

Their project for the Place Léon Aucoc in Bordeaux, France is the manifesto of this policy of minimal intervention. The brief called for the architectural "beautification" of the square. Lacaton & Vassal responded with exclusively non-architectural measures such as better street cleaning to remove dog excrement, diverting vehicular through-traffic and removing the bureaucratic hurdles that, under the pretext of safety regulations, forbade the holding of street parties, once a regular event, on the square. Asked by the city fathers what architectural suggestions they might have for making the square more beautiful they answered: "None. The square is very beautiful as it is." □

Ilka & Andreas Ruby

Palais de Tokyo, Paris, France 2002 In their re-habitation of a derelict museum building on the Seine riverbank, Lacaton & Vassal decided to intervene only for the sake of making the building technically operative again while leaving the building's architecture virtually untouched. They trusted users of the art centre to activate the space, using the square Djemaa El-Fna in Marrakech as their model: a square which is more defined by its continuously shifting-use patterns than by its surrounding architecture.

Palais de Tokyo, Paris, France 2002

Jürgen Mayer H.

It may seem to be stretching the limits somewhat to discuss a project such as Jürgen Mayer H.'s Stadthaus (district town hall) Scharnhauser Park (2001) in terms of Minimalism as this design infringes all the conventions of what is regarded as typically minimalist. Mayer H. reacts with an exorcist's *horror vacui* to the "boutique Cistercianism" (Charles Jencks) of the 1990s. He encounters the instrumentali-sation of Minimal Art as an empty—and therefore all the more effective—stage for selling goods by means of overloading them with meaning. He responds to the silence maintained by the protagonists of mainstream minimalism and their reluctance to engage in a discourse by employing an overabundance of terms and reacts to their obsessive search for authenticity, the nature and the essence of things with a playful scepticism that regards neither things nor words as self-evident. ›

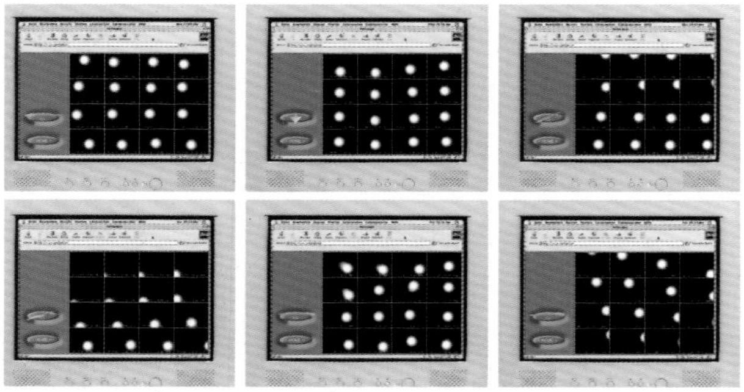

Stadthaus Scharnhauser Park (district town hall), Ostfildern, Germany 2001 Identity is a crucial issue for an area like Scharnhäuser Park which was created from scratch during the past ten years. An important element of Mayer H.'s "performative minimalism" (André Bideau) is the group of poles which mark the edge of the market place. Its dimensions and its inclincation correspond to the space under the soffit roof. Instead of flags flying in the wind, fibre optic cables are attached to the poles. Light beams are projected onto the floor. Webcams are to be installed in order to make the ever-changing pattern of the light dots available on the city's homepage.

SERVICE
BÜRGERSERVICE

Over-representation or "hyper-programming" as Mayer H. puts it highlights a problem with which minimal artists also wrestled, namely the idea that things speak for themselves. This notion lies at the root of "boutique Cistercianism". For example: in the bare interior of a salesroom by Pawson et al. only a few goods are displayed, often without any indication of their price. This indicates a fear that a label, due to its representative character, may endanger the value of the things as it implies that this value is not naturally given, is not eternal and self-evident but variable and artificially attributed. (This is comparable to the phenomenon that, at some art exhibitions, labels are moved away from the artworks for fear they could, in some way, disturb the aesthetic effect of the works). As a sign of his sceptical attitude towards what appears self-evident Mayer H. likes to entitle his Stadthaus itself "stadt.haus" (town.house). He accompanied its development with two models: the aluminium box and the e.gram. For a time the representation attracted more attention than the built project.

When we take look at his Stadthaus, built on the ruins of an American barracks as the centre of a newly established urban district, then several of those terms that form a normal part of the rhetoric employed to describe any building project can be used only in inverted commas. Terms such as "nature", "public", "transparency" and "citizen-friendly" become slogans whose meaning can be shifted back and forth as required. Staircases are stages lit-up like a television studio. The room used for marriage ceremonies is fitted out with a golden wedding dress. By means of a computer programme the administration can make it rain from the soffit of the projecting roof slab, using different "pitter-patterns". Not one of the materials he uses is authentic, even the aluminium panels of the facades are in different shades. In contrast to the naturalism of many of his colleagues, who evoke the very nature their architectures destroy as image, thus incorporating it into architecture. Mayer H.'s approach is decidedly anti-naturalistic. He brings the discussion about minimalism back to the unsolved problems of the 1960s in order to activate them anew. □

Philip Ursprung

rain code

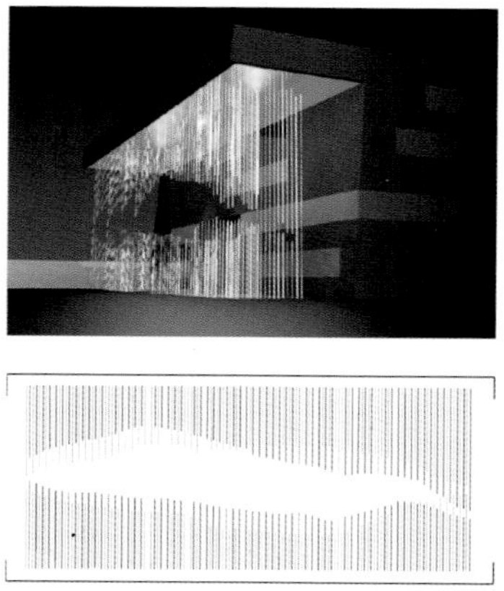

rain cave

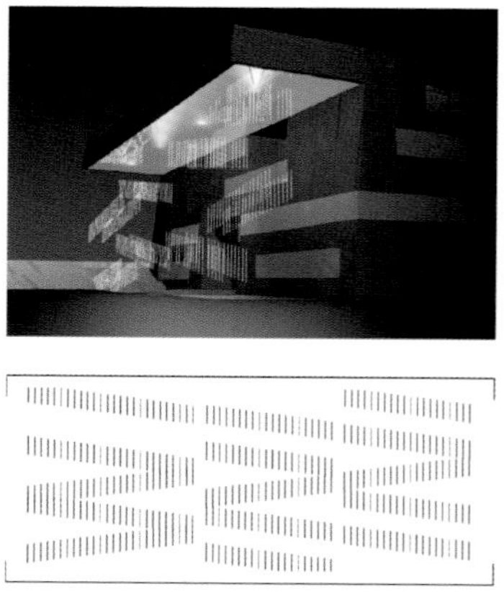

zig zag

Stadthaus Scharnhauser Park (district town hall), Ostfildern, Germany 2001 "Pitterpatterns, Studies on Falling Water" is the ironical title Mayer H. gave to a special device which enables the administration to let it rain. Traditional emblems of power such as the baroque cascades are used to distinguish the area as a public sphere. And doesn't the subject of the weather initiate most conversations between people? The (over)representation of the public sphere is also crucial for the interior where staircases are lit like the stage of a 1990s TV show. The decorative patterns of the wall-to-wall carpets are based on data-security patterns hereby producing an ironic commentary on the entanglement of the public and private sphere.

Sadar Vuga Arhitekti

Sadar Vuga's projects have a deceptive directness. It only seems that they are always filled by a central, directly communicated idea. You believe you have formed an impression of them yet the longer you look at them, the more ambivalent they become. New aspects surface, making the first impression relative and indeed often exposing it as a farce. The projects' iconic directness thus serves to manipulate perception, to lull observers into a sense of security or entice them along a false trail.

To take an example: in their National Gallery one could initially imagine distant echoes of the weighty pathos of Mies van der Rohe's glass buildings. Filling the vacant site between the two existing museum exhibition buildings, the transparent volume appears to conceal something special in its interior, something secret that could legitimise the building's spectacular dramaturgy. Once inside, however, you realise there is nothing there. Apart from the cash desk and bookshop, there are only stairs, a connecting gallery between the two old buildings and a large platform on which nothing happens. Whereas in Mies' case emptiness is used to indicate something transcendental, here it is just empty. In contrast the shell containing it is more than present. Seen from the street the structure of the building seems delicate and diaphanous, from the perspective of the interior, swivelled through 90 degrees, it becomes a densely wrought pattern of dark painted steel beams, whose perceived form changes with every step the observer takes. ›

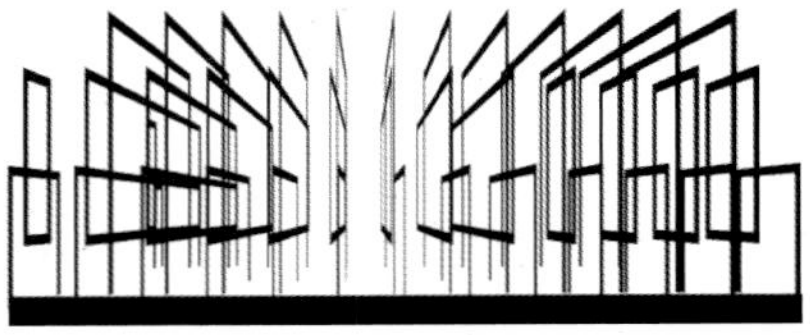

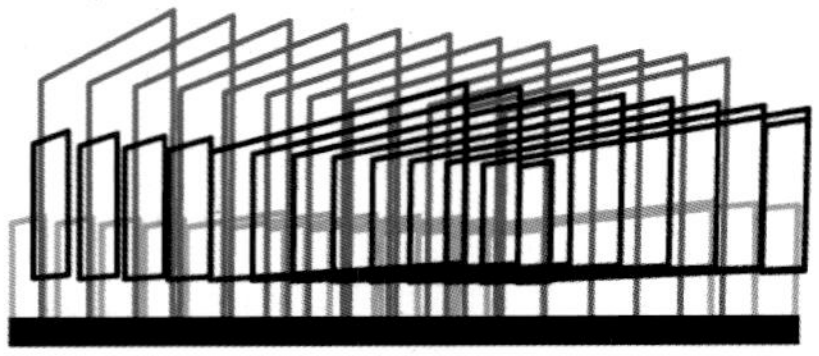

New Entrance Hall of the National Gallery, Ljubljana, Slovenia 2001
Bridging the gap between the two existing buildings of the National Gallery, its new entrance hall serves, beyond its evident function of circulation and access, primarily as an event space for gallery openings and receptions.

New Entrance Hall of the National Gallery, Ljubljana, Slovenia 2001 Besides being used for gallery openings and receptions, it is increasingly used as a stage for performances and events which the gallery rents to external users, including commercial events like fashion shows, the launching of new cars and award ceremonies. Through its strong public programme, the building has become a "city living room" where one can spend time without having the intention of visiting an exhibition.

This ambivalent corporeality of the building also characterises their project for the Shopping Center Mercator. Seen from the regional highway the red hall appears to be a smooth minimalist volume. But when you drive into the car park the skin of the building begins to break open and mutates unexpectedly into a deconstructivist facade. But this drama is dispelled equally quickly as the space behind it is only a couple of metres deep. In terms of its position it is a vestibule but atmospherically it contradicts its function as a reception area with a dense tangle of air-conditioning ducts hanging like a parasitic growth from the ceiling.

As the shopping halls beyond are kept emphatically low-key and neutral you have already forgotten the excitement of entering when you finally leave the building by a side exit only to be confronted by a completely unexpected view behind the scenes. The deconstructivist entrance volume is revealed as a Potemkinian village: an inflated front building, resembling a facade in a Western, stands in front of the flat volume of the actual supermarket which is, in fact, a converted industrial shed. ›

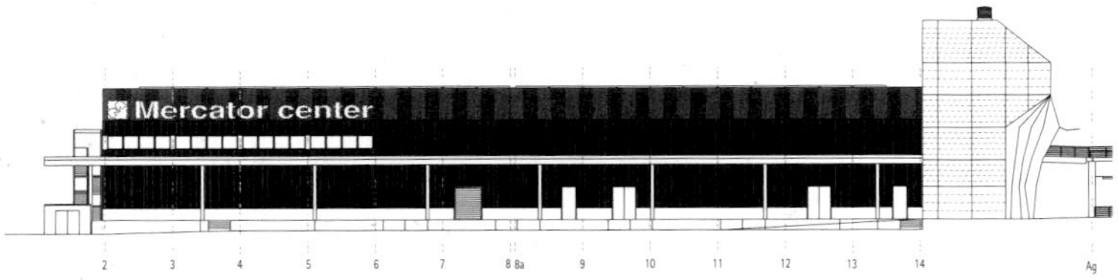

Shopping Center Mercator, Nova Gorica, Slovenia 2001 What approaching from the highway looks like a large monolith is in fact nothing but a transitional building between a two-storey parking garage and the supermarket accommodated in a converted warehouse behind it. Despite its small footprint, this bulwark structure constitutes for the most part the perceived architectural effect of the overall building and acts like a Potemkinian village of contemporary consumer culture.

The same ambivalent game with representation characterises the building for Arcadia Lightwear, a Slovenian lighting planner and light-fitting manufacturer. Instead of displaying its function outwardly with an effectively illuminated piece of architecture, the building presents itself with a deep, dark blue facade that draws the gaze into a black hole. The showroom concealed behind in a certain sense acts outwardly as a "hiding room". Only the building's recessed ground floor is covered with a shiny foil that at night reflects the light cast by the headlamps of passing cars. That is to say, the building does not light up, it allows itself to be lit up. At the same time the architecture does not make this principle its sole concept. The offices and warehouse are not incorporated in the box but are oriented towards the rear and allow themselves to be recognised as what they are. In contrast to mainstream minimalism Sadar Vuga are not primarily interested in the creation of an aura around their architecture but in showing how such an aura is produced. For this reason their buildings always contain both the illusion and the key to dispelling it. □

Ilka & Andreas Ruby

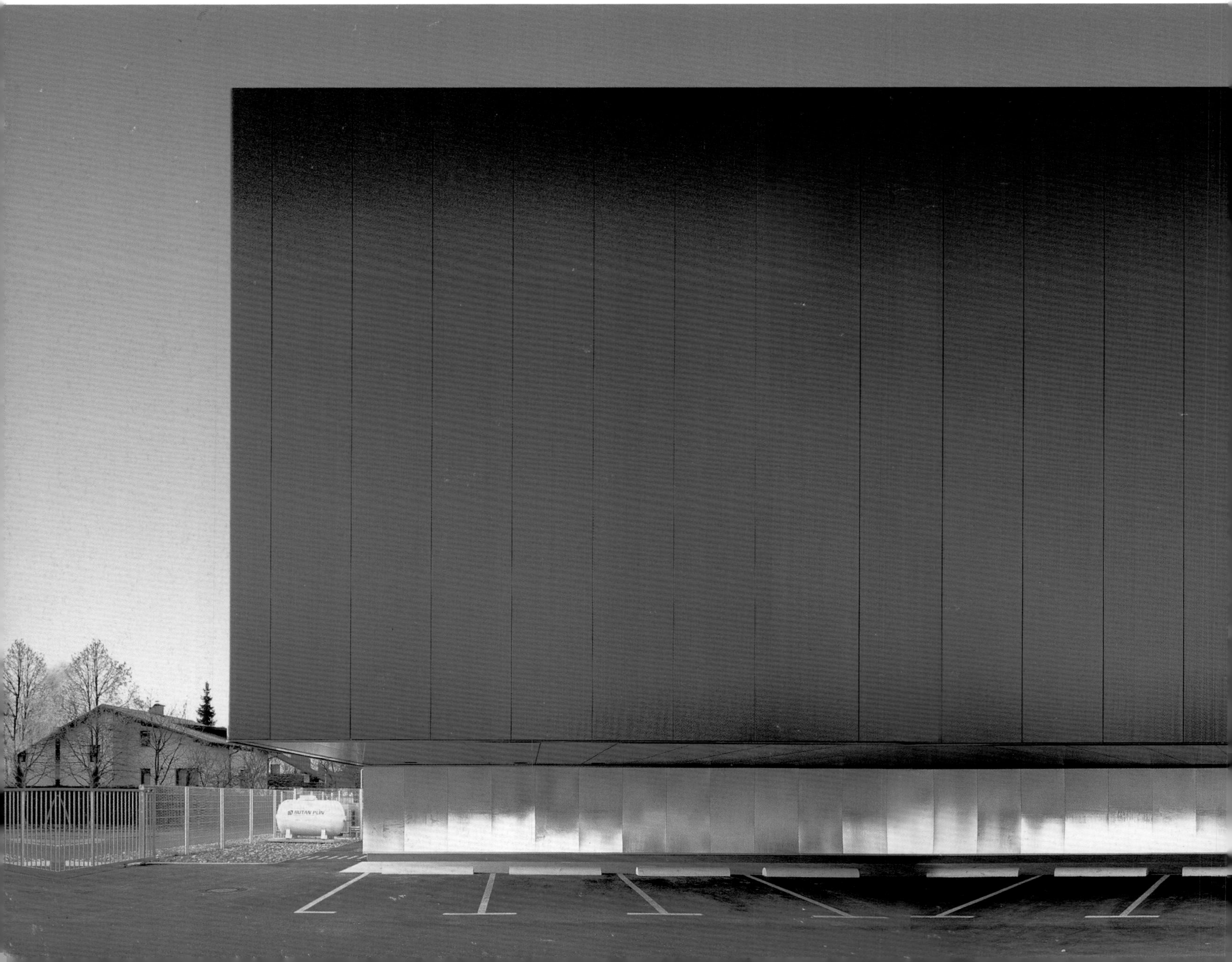

Arcadia Lightwear Office and Exhibition Building, Ljubljana, Slovenia 2000 Manifesting itself largely by a dark volume hovering in mid-air, this building is actually the headquarters of a light manufacturer. The black box contains a showroom for lighting equipment. It is continued throughout the circulation ramps in the middle of the building which provide access to the offices at the back and the apartment on the top.

Zaha Hadid

While there can be no doubt that this project represents a rather unique stance in Zaha Hadid's oeuvre it nevertheless extrapolates a tendency that reoccurs throughout her work, i.e. she does not view buildings as isolated elements but develops them as part of a broader manipulation of the site topography. This manipulation is generally conducted from a bird's-eye vantage point, visualising the ground as a gigantic mass. At the same time the bird's-eye view means that the building is thought of as something that lowers itself onto the ground from above rather than growing out of the earth. It lands. The act of landing causes a topographical reorganisation of the ground out of which the building is developed. Its origins in its spatial context often remain hidden as in most cases only the building itself is given a designed form, the surrounding external space remaining unshaped.

In Strasbourg however Hadid was able to demonstrate with an unparalleled degree of clarity the often-concealed way her architecture charges its surroundings. Here the building itself—a tram terminus with roofs to shelter people waiting for a tram from the elements—forms only a minor part of the project. The major part is, on the other hand, laid out as an infrastructural landscape formed by the white stripes defining the parking spaces and the inclined lamp-posts in the car park. In addition, a monumental light-coloured surface spreads across the site. When seen from the perspective of a pedestrian its significance is not entirely clear but a bird's-eye view reveals that this coloured surface also spreads over the roofs of the station. ›

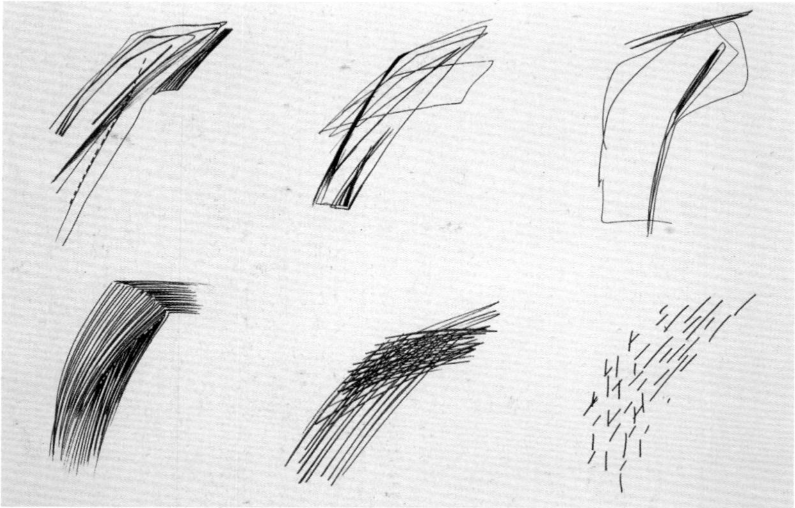

Terminus Hoenheim-Nord, Strasbourg, France 2001 With this park-and-ride facility in the north of Strasbourg, Zaha Hadid designed an unprecedented scape-set for the fluid intermingling of people, cars and trams. The various facilities accommodating these different flows are conceived as a single interwoven plateau which both blends and contrasts with the surrounding suburban landscape.

The shadow cast by the roof onto the light-coloured asphalt gives the surface of the ground a visual depth reminiscent of a number of Land Art works (e.g. those by Michael Heizer) which, for their part, can often be seen in their entirety only from the air. Land Art also relates to an aspect of minimalism that has hardly ever been pursued by the architectural variation of this movement: the way sculpture became independent, in terms of scale, of its context and as a consequence constantly conquered new spaces of reference and ultimately led, via stops in galleries, museums and public space, to landscape. In a related way Hadid oversteps the architectural framework of her project by allowing the building's footprint to be absorbed by the major form of the light-coloured ground. This expansion of the object into the landscape is continued to include the handling of the lamp-posts in the car park, the angle they make taking up the line of the raking supports to the terminus-building roof.

The aerial view, visually suggestive of a plan, finally reveals that the phenomenological complexity which the car park unfolds at ground level with its forest of lines and points is, in fact, based on a rather simple geometric pattern that appears to transfer Walter de Maria's *Lightning Field* to Strasbourg in a single graceful movement. □

Ilka & Andreas Ruby

Terminus Hoenheim-Nord, Strasbourg, France 2001
Varying between white and grey, the demarcation lines of the parking spaces produce a lively pattern on the black tarmac. The vertical lighting posts enhance this dancing movement on the ground while establishing an elevated perceptual field of reference through the carpet of lights against the background of the nocturnal sky.

Diller + Scofidio

For the Arteplage Yverdon-les-Bains of the Swiss national exhibition 2002, the *Expo.02*, Diller & Scofidio designed the project Blur, which under the name "clowd" became a symbol of the exhibition. The technical expenditure was minimal; basically it was a giant sprinkler erected above the lake that sprayed what seemed like lake water in innumerable fine drops (in fact, due to the pollution of the lake drinking water was used). Depending on the weather the moisture either hovered above the lake in the form of a dense cloud or drifted like a mist over the shore.

Initially it was planned to equip Blur with various attractions such as video projections and a sushi bar and to provide visitors with interactive rain capes, so-called "braincoats". For financial reasons only the Angel Bar on the upper deck of the Blur was realised in which mineral water from around the globe was available. In addition a lightshow at night presented the cloud in blue and yellow light. It was precisely this lack of attractions that made the project so unique. In contrast to the traditional pavilions at world exhibitions in which the senses are flooded with images, sounds and information, in the interior of the Blur there was literally nothing to be seen. Depending on the weather the visitors lost sight of each other and at times it was even difficult to make out one's hand in front of one's face. All visual and acoustic references were erased on entering the mist and the senses were blurred. In the architects' own words: "What remains is an optical white-out and the white noise of the nozzles." ›

Blur, Arteplage Yverdon-les-Bains, Switzerland 2002 The lightweight Tensegrity structure of Blur measures 100 metres wide by 65 metres deep and 25 metres high. Water is shot through a dense array of 31,000 high-pressure mist nozzles.

Blur, Arteplage Yverdon-les-Bains, Switzerland 2002 Among the original proposals for activities within Blur, only the Angel Bar was eventually realized. Various mineral waters from around the world were available. Initially, the architects had planned that water from different global sources—distilled water, rainwater, glacial and polar water as well as municipal tap water from international cities—be obtainable. In the words of the architects: "The public is invited to drink the building." Another early project deals with "braincoats", i.e. raincoats bearing the character profiles of the persons wearing them. The coats were supposed to be interactive. Visitors meeting in the fog would have had their braincoats reacted to each other, changing in colour and thus indicating the degree of affinity. A perfect match would have been a red glow, much like involuntary blushing. Due to the lack of funds, this project could unfortunately not be realized.

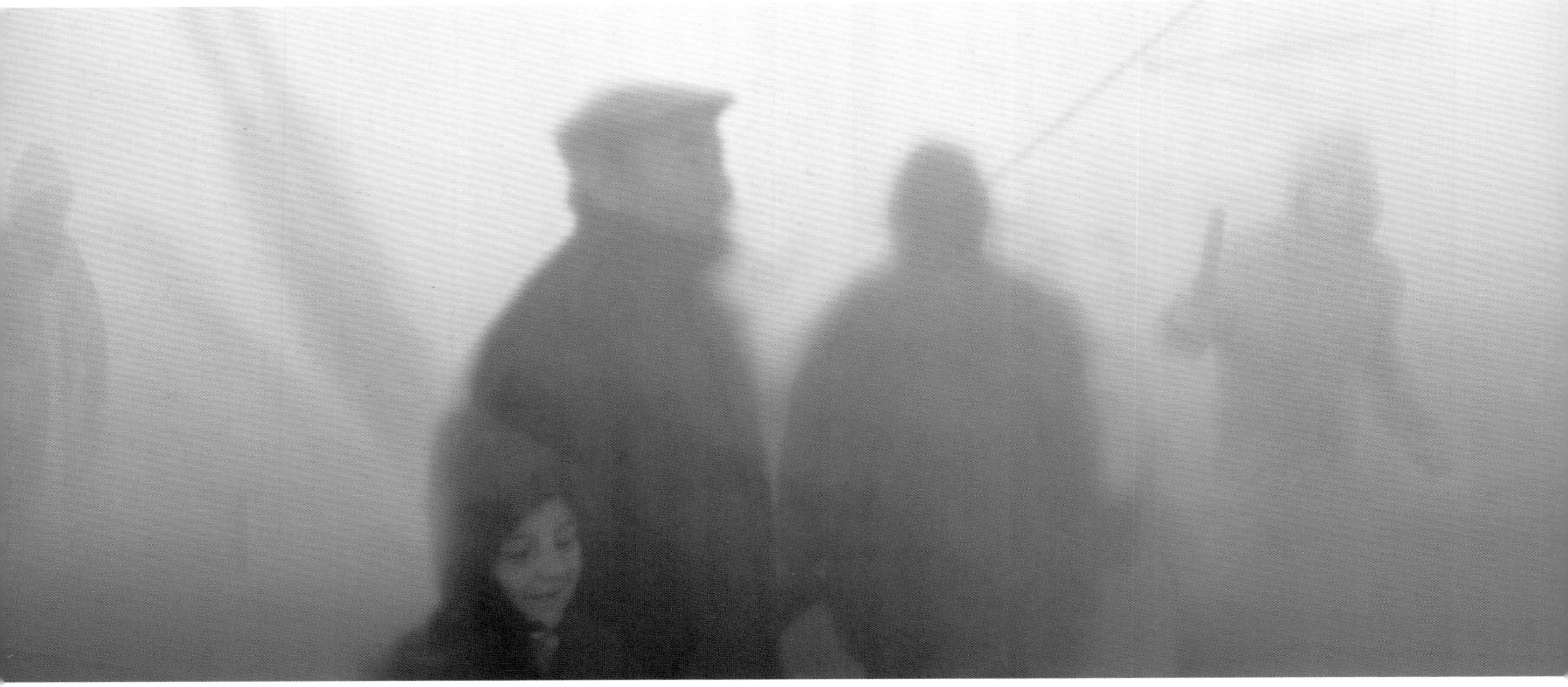

Blur, Arteplage Yverdon-les-Bains, Switzerland 2002 Open to all kind of interpretations and associations, Blur became one of the main attractions of the Swiss national exhibition, the *Expo.02*. As a landmark it recalls the long history of world fair exhibitions, from the *montgolfière* which was hovering over the Première exposition des produits de l'industrie française in Paris in 1798 to Buckminster Fuller's American Pavilion at the *Expo 67* in Montréal, and Fujiko Nakaya's fog installation on the Pepsi Cola Pavilion at the 1970 Osaka World's Fair. Nakaya was acutually an advisor to Diller + Scofidio on technical and aesthetic matters.

This nothingness, this elimination of sensory impressions apparently so irritated the management of the *Expo.02* that, perhaps out of fear that the visitors might infect themselves with an uncontrollable form of nihilism, they commissioned Christian Marclay to install a sound installation. This *horror vacui* on the part of an institution that feels committed to the transmittal of content and the production of meaning is most interesting. It indicates the potential of an architecture that does not mediate, that does not establish a sense of community, that at certain moments interrupts the predominance of the visual. It also shows the possibilities of an architectural position (that can be seen as threatening or welcome, depending on one's viewpoint), which works with literalness, evaporation and expansion rather than abstraction, compression and reduction and which articulates entropy rather than suppressing it. □

Philip Ursprung

Blur, Arteplage Yverdon-les-Bains, Switzerland 2002 Depending on the humidity of the air and the direction of the wind, the shape of Blur constantly changed. At some moments it spilled over the so-called Arteplage, the location of the other pavilions and attractions, thus announcing its presence as a change of atmosphere before it could actually be seen.

Architects

Tadao Ando Architect & Associates
Osaka, Japan

Wiel Arets Architect & Associates
Maastricht, The Netherlands
arets@wxs.nl

Shigeru Ban Architects
Tokyo, Japan
sba@tokyo.email.ne.jp

BeL
Anne-Julchen Bernhardt, Jörg Leeser
Cologne, Germany
www.rationator.org

Claus en Kaan Architecten
Felix Claus, Kees Kaan
Amsterdam and Rotterdam, The Netherlands
www.clausenkaan.nl

Diener & Diener Architekten
Roger Diener
Basle, Switzerland
www.dienerdiener.ch

Diller + Scofidio
Elizabeth Diller, Ricardo Scofidio
New York, USA
www.dillerscofidio.com

Gigon/Guyer
Annette Gigon, Mike Guyer
Zurich, Switzerland
www.gigon-guyer.ch

Zaha Hadid Architects
London, England
www.zaha-hadid.com

Herzog & de Meuron
Jacques Herzog, Pierre de Meuron, Harry Gugger,
Christine Binswanger
Basel, Switzerland
info@herzogdemeuron.ch

Atelier Krischanitz
Adolf Krischanitz
Vienna, Austria
www.krischanitz.at

José Rafael Moneo Arquitecto
José Rafael Moneo Vallés
Madrid, Spain

Lacaton & Vassal Architectes
Anne Lacaton, Jean Philippe Vassal
Paris, France
lacaton.vassal@wanadoo.fr

J. Mayer H. Architekten
Jürgen Mayer H.
Berlin, Germany
www.jmayerh.de

Morger & Degelo Architekten
Meinrad Morger, Heinrich Degelo, Benjamin Theiler
Basel, Switzerland
mail@morger-degelo.ch

OMA Office for Metropolitan Architecture
Rem Koolhaas, Ole Scheeren, Ellen van Loon
Rotterdam, The Netherlands
www.oma.nl

Dominique Perrault Architecte
Paris, France
www.perraultarchitecte.com

R&Sie...
François Roche, Stephanie Lavaux
Paris, France
www.new-territories.com

Sadar Vuga Arhitekti
Jurij Sadar, Boštjan Vuga
Ljubljana, Slovenia
www.sadarvuga.com

SANAA
Kazuyo Sejima + Ryue Nishizawa
Tokyo, Japan
www.sanaa.co.jp

Bibliography

General

Architectural Design, 7/8, 1994 (Aspects of Minimal Architecture).
Architectural Design, 5/6, 1999 (Aspects of Minimal Architecture II).
Gregory Battcock (ed.), *Minimal Art, A Critical Anthology*, New York 1968, (reprint, with an introduction by Anne Wagner, Berkeley 1995).
Franco Bertoni, *Minimalist Architecture*, Basel, Boston, Berlin 2002.
Franco Bertoni, *Claudio Silvestrin*, Florence 1999.
Hans Frei, "Leave the Channels—follow the Roots", *Arch+*, 129/130, 1995, pp. 103–106.
Lotus International, 81, 1994 (Neominimalismo).
Matiere d'art. Architecture contemporaine en Suisse / A Matter of Art. Contemporary Architecture in Switzerland, exhib. catalogue, Centre Culturel Suisse Paris, Basel, Boston, Berlin 2001.
James Meyer (ed.), *Minimalism*, London 2000.
James Meyer, *Minimalism, Art and Polemics in the Sixties*, New Haven 2001.
Minimalismos, un signo de los tiempos, exhib. catalogue, Museo Nacional Centro de Arte Reina Sofia, Madrid 2001.
Josep Maria Montaner, "Minimalisms", *El Croquis*, 62/63, 1993.
John Pawson, *Minimal*, London 1998.
Rassegna, 36/4, 1988 (Minimal).
Vittorio E. Savi and Josep M. Montaner (eds.), *Less is more. Minimalism in Architecture and the other Arts,* exhib. catalogue, Barcelona 1996.
Dietmar Steiner, "Promotional Architecture", *Architectural Design*, 6, 2000, pp. 20–24.
Gregor Stemmrich (ed.), *Minimal Art, Eine kritische Retrospekive*, Dresden 1995.
Techniques & Architecture, 423, 1996 (Tendance Minimale).
Philip Ursprung, "Der Triumph des Minimalismus", *White Fire–Flying Man. Amerikanische Kunst 1959–1999 in Basel*, Katharina Schmidt and Philip Ursprung (eds.), exhib. catalogue, Museum für Gegenwartskunst Basel, Basel 1999, pp. 125–131.
Anatxu Zabalbeascoa and Javier Rodríguez Marcos, *Minimalisms*, Barcelona 2000.

Tadao Ando

Beyond Minimalism: The Architecture of Tadao Ando, exhib. catalogue, Royal Academy of Arts, London 1998.
Francesco Dal Co, *Tadao Ando. Complete Works*, Milan 1994, London 1995.
Philip Jodidio, *Tadao Ando*, Cologne 2001.
Koji Taki, *Minimalism or Monotonality? A Contextual analysis of Tadao Ando's Method*, New York 1984.

Wiel Arets

Wiel Arets, *Maastricht Academy for the Arts and Architecture*, Rotterdam 1994.
Jos Bosman (ed.), *Wiel Arets: Strange Bodies/Fremdkörper*, Basel, Boston, Berlin 1996.
Xavier Costa (ed.) and Hélène Binet (photographs), *Wiel Arets*, Barcelona, Basel, Boston, 2002.

Shigeru Ban

Eugenia Bell (ed.), *Shigeru Ban*, Princeton, New Jersey 2001.

Claus en Kaan

a+u, 382, 2002 (Claus en Kaan Architecten).

beauftragt. Claus en Kaan Architecten, exhib. catalogue, Aedes, Berlin 2002.

Hans Ibelings (ed.), *Claus en Kaan, Building*, Rotterdam 2001.

Diener & Diener

Roger Diener and Martin Steinmann, *Das Haus und die Stadt / The House and the City. Diener & Diener – Städtebauliche Arbeiten/Urban Studies*, exhib. catalogue, Architekturgalerie Luzern, Lucerne, Basel 1995.

Diller + Scofidio

Elizabeth Diller, Ricardo Scofidio, *Blur, The making of nothing*, New York 2002.

Richard D. Phillips, Aaron Betsky, K. Michael Hays et al., *Scanning: The Aberrant Architectures of Diller + Scofidio*, exhib. catalogue, The Whitney Museum of American Art, New York 2003.

Philip Ursprung, "Weißes Rauschen: Elisabeth Diller und Richard Scofidios Blur Building und die räumliche Logik der jüngsten Architektur", *Kritische Berichte, Zeitschrift für Kunst- und Kulturwissenschaften*, 29, vol. 3, 2001, pp. 5–15.

Gigon/Guyer

J. Christoph Bürkle (ed.), *Gigon Guyer Architekten, Arbeiten 1989–2000*, Sulgen 2000.

El Croquis, 102, 2000 (Annette Gigon + Mike Guyer, 1989–2000).

Zaha Hadid

Hélène Binet, Lars Müller, *Architecture of Zaha Hadid in Photographs by Helene Binet*, Baden 2001.

Zaha Hadid, Aaron Betsky, *Zaha Hadid: The Complete Buildings and Projects*, London 1998.

Herzog & de Meuron

a+u, February 2002 special issue, 2002.

El Croquis, 60/84, 2000 (Herzog & de Meuron).

Herzog & de Meuron, Eberswalde Library, special issue of *Architecture Landscape Urbanism*, 3, Architectural Association School of Architecture, London, 2000.

Edelbert Köb (ed.), *Herzog & de Meuron, Sammlung Goetz*, Kunsthaus Bregenz, archiv kunst architektur, Stuttgart 1995.

Gerhard Mack, *Herzog & de Meuron, Das Gesamtwerk/The Complete Works*, 3 vols, vol. 1, 1978–88, vol. 2, 1989–91, vol. 3, 1992–96, Basel 1996–2000.

Philip Ursprung (ed.), *Herzog & de Meuron, Natural History*, exhib. catalogue, Canadian Centre for Architecture Montréal, Baden 2002.

Adolf Krischanitz

Edelbert Köb (ed.), *Krischanitz, Federle. Neue Welt Schule*, Kunsthaus Bregenz, archiv kunst architektur, Stuttgart 1994.

Adolf Krischanitz, architect: buildings and projects 1986–1998, Basel, Boston, Berlin 1998.

Lacaton & Vassal

Marie-Ange Brayer, Béatrice Simonot (eds.), *Contextes*, catalogue of the French Pavilion at the 8th Venice Biennale International Exhibition of Architecture 2002, Orléans 2002, pp. 96–99.

Ilka & Andreas Ruby, "Beyond Form. Notes on the Work of Lacaton & Vassal", *2G*, 21, 2002, pp. 4–19.

Hubert Tonka, Jeanne-Marie Sens (eds.), *Une Maison particulière à Floirac (Gironde) de Anne Lacaton & Jean-Philippe Vassal*, Paris 1994.

J. Mayer H.

André Bideau, "Performativer Minimalismus, Das Stadthaus Scharnhauser Park bei Stuttgart", *Neue Zürcher Zeitung*, 31, 7 February 2002, p. 79.

Albert Ferré, "Überrepräsentation von Öffentlichkeit", *Werk, Bauen und Wohnen*, 5, 2002, pp. 48–53 (original english text on www.werkbauenundwohnen.ch).

Philip Ursprung, "The Transparance of the Model as the Model of Transparency, Jürgen Mayer Hermann's–e.gram", *Daidalos* 74, 2000, pp. 62–65.

José Rafael Moneo

El Croquis, 98, 2000 (Rafael Moneo 1995–2000).

El Croquis, 64, 1994 (Rafael Moneo 1990/1994).

Morger & Degelo

J. Christoph Bürkle (ed.), *Morger & Degelo Architekten*, Sulgen 2000.

Kunstmuseum Liechtenstein, Morger Degelo Kerez Architekten, Baden 2000.

OMA Office for Metropolitan Architecture

Patrizio Bertelli, Rem Koolhaas, Michael Kubo (eds.), *Rem Koolhaas: Projects for Prada Part 1*, Milan 2001.

Chuihua Judy Chung, Jeffrey Inaba, Rem Koolhaas, Sze Tsung Leong (eds.), *Shopping*, Cologne 2001.

Rem Koolhaas, Chuihua Judy Chung, Jeffrey Inaba, Sze Tsung Leong (eds.), *Great Leap Forward*, Cologne 2001.

Dominique Perrault

El Croquis, 104, 2001 (Dominique Perrault, The violence of neutral).

Dominique Perrault, Architect, Basel 1999.

Dominique Perrault, Progetti e architetture, con uns saggio di Laurent Stalder, Milan 2000.

R&Sie

Marie-Ange Brayer, Béatrice Simonot (eds.), Archilab 2001, Orléans, 2001, pp. 28–31, 218–225.

Mutations @morphes. R, DSV & Sie, exhib. catalogue, Frac Centre, Orléans 1998.

Ilka & Andreas Ruby "Informed Surfaces. Continuity as the Narration of the Nineties", *Werk, Bauen + Wohnen*, 11, 2002, pp. 39–45.

Sadar Vuga Arhitekti

Marie-Ange Brayer, Frederic Migayrou, *Archilab 2000,* Orléans 2000, p. 202–210.

Zaha Hadid, Patrik Schumacher (ed.), *Latent Utopias. Experiments within Contemporary Architecture*, exhib. catalogue, 2002, pp. 232–235.

Hrvoje Njiric, "Neo-modern imagery. Spatial diagram and spatial aesthetics in the new Slovenian Chamber of Commerce", *Werk, Bauen + Wohnen*, 12/2000, pp. 22–27.

SANAA / Kazuyo Sejima + Ryue Nishizawa

El Croquis, 77 (I), 1996 (Kazuyo Sejima 1988–1996).

El Croquis, 99, 2000 (Kazuyo Sejima + Ryue Nishizawa 1995–2000).

Author Biographies

Andreas Ruby studied History of Art at the University of Cologne in Germany before undertaking postgraduate studies on the Theory and History of Architecture at the Ecole Spéciale d'Architecture Paris with Paul Virilio and at Columbia University in New York with Bernard Tschumi. **Ilka Ruby** studied Architecture at RWTH Aachen, Germany. After practicing as an architect for some years, she now works as a graphic designer, editor and writer. In 2001, they set up their joint editorial agency to publish architectural books and magazines as well as writing essays on contemporary architecture. www.textbild.com

Angeli Sachs is an art historian and editor for architecture and design, based in Munich. She has collaborated and curated for the Deutsches Architektur Museum in Frankfurt/Main and the Institute for the History and Theory of Architecture at the Federal Institute of Technology in Zurich. She has published widely in the fields of art and architecture of the 20th century.

Philip Ursprung taught at several universities in Switzerland and Germany, and is now professor of Contemporary Art History at the Institute for the History and Theory of Architecture at the Federal Institute of Technology in Zurich. He is guest curator at the Canadian Centre for Architecture in Montréal, Canada, and has a number of publications on art and architecture of the 19th and 20th century to his name.

The publisher and the authors would like to express their utmost gratitude to all of those who contributed to this book. The individual architectural practices were extremely helpful in providing material and information.

Illustration Credits

p. 6 (left) Rudolph Burckhardt/Art Donald Judd Estate/VG Bild-Kunst, Bonn 2003

p. 6 (right) VG Bild-Kunst, Bonn 2003

p. 8 (left) Estate of Dan Flavin/VG Bild-Kunst, Bonn 2003

p. 8 (right), 9 (top), 10 (right) VG Bild-Kunst, Bonn 2003

p. 9 (bottom) Courtesy Paula Cooper Gallery, New York

p. 11 Philip Ursprung/Art Donald Judd Estate/VG Bild-Kunst, Bonn 2003

p. 12 The Jewish Museum, New York

p. 16 (left) Christoph Kicherer, Paris

p. 16 (right) Luís Seixa Ferreira Alves, Porto

p. 17 Heinrich Helfenstein, Zurich

p. 18 (left) Ruedi Walti, Basel

p. 18 (right) artur/Zooey Braun, Cologne

p. 19 Hisao Suzuki, Barcelona

p. 20 (all) Tadao Ando, Osaka

p. 21 Christoph Kicherer, Paris

p. 22 (left), 23 (left) Margherita Spiluttini, Vienna

p. 22 (right), 23 (right) Philip Ursprung, Zurich

p. 24 (left) OMA, Rotterdam

p. 24 (right) Werner Hutmacher, Fribourg/VG Bild-Kunst, Bonn 2003

p. 25 Herzog & de Meuron, Basel

p. 30 (bottom left), 32, 33 Mitsuo Matsuoka/Shinkenchiku-sha, Tokyo, courtesy Tadao Ando

p. 30 (bottom right), 31, 35 (two sketches left) Tadao Ando, Osaka

p. 34–35, 35 (top right), 36 (all), 37 Makoto Yamamori/Shinkenchiku-sha, Tokyo, courtesy Tadao Ando

p. 38, 39, 40/41, 43 Margherita Spiluttini, Vienna

p. 42 (sketch and drawing) Herzog & de Meuron, Basel

p. 44, 45, 46, 47 Heinrich Helfenstein, Zurich, courtesy Gigon/Guyer

p. 48, 49 (all), 50/51, 52/53, 53 Margherita Spiluttini, Vienna, courtesy Atelier Krischanitz

p. 54–55 Ruedi Walti, Basel

p. 56, 57, 58/59 Thomas Flechtner, Sagne, courtesy Morger & Degelo

p. 60, 61 Roland Halbe, Stuttgart

p. 62, 63 Christian Richters, Münster, courtesy Diener & Diener

p. 64/65, 66/67 (all) Diener & Diener, Basel

p. 70/71, 72/73, 74/75 Margherita Spiluttini, Vienna

p. 74 (drawings) Herzog & de Meuron, Basel

p. 76/77 (bottom), 78 Roland Halbe, Stuttgart

p. 77 (top left and right), 79 David Cardelús, Barcelona

p. 80/81, 81 Hisao Suzuki, Barcelona

p. 82–83, 85, 88/89 Hélène Binet, London

p. 84, 86, 87 Kim Zwarts, Maastricht

p. 90, 91, 92 (all), 93 Ger van der Vlugt, Amsterdam, courtesy Claus en Kaan

p. 94 (all), 95, 96/97, 97, 98, 98/99 Christian Richters, Münster, courtesy Claus en Kaan

p. 100/101, 101 (all), 102/103, 103, 104/105 George Fessy/VG Bild-Kunst, Bonn 2003, courtesy Dominique Perrault

p. 104 (sketches) Dominique Perrault, Paris

p. 106, 106/107, 108 (bottom left, right), 109, 110/111, 111, 112, 113 (all), Shinkenchiku-sha, Tokyo

p. 108 (drawing) SANAA, Tokyo

p. 114, 114/115, 115 (bottom), 116/117 Marc Räder, Berlin, courtesy BeL

p. 115 (photographs top middle, top right) Ilka & Andreas Ruby, textbild, Cologne

p. 115 (top left, three drawings) BeL, Cologne

p. 118 OMA, Rotterdam

p. 119 Guggenheim Hermitage/OMA 2001, VG Bild-Kunst, Bonn 2003, photograph: Guggenheim

p. 122, 123, 124/125, 126, 126/127, 128/129, 129 Hiroyuki Hirai, Tokyo, courtesy Shigeru Ban

p. 130 OMA, Rotterdam

p. 131, 132/133 Armin Linke, Milan

p. 134 (all), 135, 136, 137, 138/139, 139 (all) R&Sie..., Paris

p. 140–41, 142, 143 Lacaton & Vassal, Paris

p. 144 (all), 145 (all), 146/147 Philippe Ruault, Nantes, courtesy Lacaton & Vassal

p. 148 (photograph bottom), 151 Ilka & Andreas Ruby, Cologne

p. 148 (rendering) J. Mayer H., Berlin

p. 149 David Franck, Ostfildern

p. 150 (renderings) J. Mayer H., Berlin

p. 152 (drawings), 157 (top right) Sadar Vuga, Ljubljana

p. 152 (bottom), 153, 154/155, 156/157, 157 (top left), 158/159, 159 (all) Hisao Suzuki, Barcelona, courtesy Sadar Vuga

p. 160 (sketches, image) Zaha Hadid, London

p. 160/161 Airdiasol/Rothan, Strasbourg

p. 162, 162/163 Hélène Binet, London, courtesy Zaha Hadid

p. 164 Dirk Hebel, courtesy Diller + Scofidio

p. 165 (all), 166/167 (all), 168 (left) Diller + Scofidio, New York

p. 168–69 Beat Widmer, courtesy Diller + Scofidio

Front and back cover: © Heinrich Helfenstein, detail of Gigon/Guyer's Switching Station in Zurich, Switzerland 1996–99, see pp. 47
Frontispiece: © Margherita Spiluttini, detail of Herzog & de Meuron's Signal Box, Auf dem Wolf, Basel, Switzerland 1989–94, see pp. 70–71

Prestel Verlag
Königinstrasse 9, D-80539 Munich
Tel. +49 (89) 38 17 09-0
Fax +49 (89) 38 17 09-35

Prestel Publishing Ltd.
4 Bloomsbury Place, London WC1A 2QA
Tel. +44 (20) 7323-5004
Fax +44 (20) 7636-8004

Prestel Publishing
175 Fifth Avenue, Suite 402,
New York, N.Y. 10010
Tel. +1 (212) 995-2720
Fax +1 (212) 995-2733

www.prestel.com

The Library of Congress Control Number: 2003102933

Die Deutsche Bibliothek holds a record of this publication in Die Deutsche Nationalbibliografie; detailed bibliographical data can be found under: http://dnb.dde.de

Prestel books are available worldwide. Please contact your nearest bookseller or one of the above addresses for information concerning your local distributor.

Translated from the German by: James Roderick O'Donovan, Vienna
Series concept: Angeli Sachs
Editorial direction: Angeli Sachs, Curt Holtz
Editorial Assistance: Sabine Schmid
Picture Research: Sabine Schmid, Birgit Schmolke, James Young
Design and layout: WIGEL, Munich
Origination: ReproLine, Munich
Printing and binding: EBS, Verona

Printed in Italy on acid-free paper.

ISBN 3-7913-2859-X